# A Conversation Book

# Book I

# A Conversation Book:
# English in Everyday Life

## second edition

**Tina Kasloff Carver**
**Sandra Douglas Fotinos**

Northern Essex Community College
*Haverhill, Massachusetts*

*Illustrated by*
Paula Tatarunis

Prentice Hall Regents, Englewood Cliffs, NJ 07632

*Library of Congress Cataloging-in-Publication Data*

Carver, Tina Kasloff (date)
   A conversation book.

   1. English language—Conversation and phrase books.
   2. English language—Text-books for foreign speakers.
   I. Fotinos, Sandra Douglas (date).  II. Title.
PE1131.C43 1985     428.3′4     84-18290
ISBN  0-13-172362-6  (v. 1)


Editorial/production supervision and
   interior design: Lisa A. Domínguez
Cover design: Debra Watson
Manufacturing buyer: Harry P. Baisley
Page layout: Diane Koromhas and Steven Frim

Printed in the United States of America

10  9  8

ISBN 0-13-172362-6    01

Prentice-Hall International (UK) Limited, *London*
Prentice-Hall of Australia Pty. Limited, *Sydney*
Editora Prentice-Hall do Brasil, Ltda., *Rio de Janeiro*
Prentice-Hall Canada Inc., *Toronto*
Prentice-Hall Hispanoamericana, S.A., *Mexico*
Prentice-Hall of India Private Limited, *New Delhi*
Prentice-Hall of Japan, Inc., *Tokyo*
Prentice-Hall of Southeast Asia Pte. Ltd., *Singapore*
Whitehall Books Limited, *Wellington, New Zealand*

*To our children:*

**Jeffrey**      **Christina**
**Brian**        **Elizabeth**
**Daniel**       **Paul**

*who grew up with the first edition and who provided us with invaluable suggestions and assistance on the second.*

# Contents

### Competency Objectives

1. Self identification
   - give and respond to simple greetings
   - give address and phone number
2. Express feelings and states of being
3. Understand and respond to simple commands
4. Identify articles of clothing
5. Identify colors

### Competency Objectives

1. Identify parts of the body
2. Tell time in minutes and hours
3. Discuss daily routine
4. Identify members of immediate and extended family
5. Identify and count American money

### Competency Objectives

1. Identify rooms and furniture
2. Associate activities with rooms of the house
3. Identify landmarks in the neighborhood
4. Discuss problems with neighbors/solutions to problems
5. Discuss work associated with the home (inside and outside)
6. Identify animals (domesticated, farm)
7. Identify common tools and discuss their uses in repairs
8. Discuss insurance and its importance

### Competency Objectives

1. Identify time in terms of days, dates, months, and years
2. Identify holidays and discuss their significance
3. Discuss seasons of the year and activities associated with each
4. Identify articles of clothing for each season

### Competency Objectives

1. Identify common foods
2. Differentiate between prices and stores for food (comparison shopping, supermarket, grocer, discount, etc.)
3. Identify and discuss stores: (department, specialty, discount) and items purchased in each
4. Talk about American sizes and how to request size
5. Discuss credit
6. Discuss how to save money when shopping

### Competency Objectives

1. Learn to use the coin telephone
2. Learn to make local and long distance calls
3. Learn to use the telephone directory
4. Learn to request information, report emergencies, place orders
5. Identify and locate community services
6. Learn vocabulary and procedures for:
   - registering children at school
   - doing transactions at the post office
   - asking for things at the market
   - requesting information at the hospital
   - correcting a mistake at the bank
   - asking for something at the library
   - ordering at a restaurant
   - asking for service at a gas station
7. Discuss public transportation and travel
8. Learn vocabulary for and discuss cars and their care

### Competency Objectives

1. Identify jobs and locations
2. Complete a job application
3. Identify and discuss job benefits
4. Identify and discuss deductions and taxes
5. Discuss job loss and how to find a job

## Health      8

## Competency Objectives

1. Identify parts of the body (inside)
2. Discuss ways to maintain good health
3. Describe common health problems
4. Make medical and dental appointments
5. Discuss accidents and emergencies
6. Identify common hospital signs
7. Fill out medical forms

## Leisure      9

## Competency Objectives

1. Identify and discuss leisure activities

## Appendix

# Introduction

The goals of this book are to generate student-centered conversations and to build core vocabulary. When we wrote the first edition of the Conversation Books in 1974, our intent was to provide springboards for practicing idiomatic English conversation, focusing on everyday situations that students are likely to encounter in an English-speaking milieu. We felt that student-centered conversations based on everyday, real situations were more likely to produce natural language than the tightly controlled grammar-reading-dialog orientation so extensively used in the texts of that time. Since then, through our years of teaching conversation classes as well as our discussions with ESL/EFL teachers who teach this skill, we've concluded the following:

**1.** To teach true conversation (to teach anything!) there should be a true regard for the students' affective as well as cognitive learning. When students feel invested personally in a classroom that validates their lives, interests and real world, they learn faster and retain more because what they are learning is meaningful and pertinent to them.

**2.** Cross-cultural communication is an integrative part of the process. Students learning a second language must learn the cultural assumptions and expectations implicit in communication exchanges of the language, or the language learning is merely a lesson in mechanics.

**3.** Students will naturally begin to talk when they have something to say. If indeed, we are teaching true conversation based on the students' lives, each student becomes a unique resource in class. Student-centered conversation, by focusing on students' knowledge and experience, permits the teacher as facilitator, to tap into this resource, affirming the value of each individual in the class. Teachers in the student-centered class thus serve as resource facilitators as well as frequent participants, helping students learn *how* to say what they want to say, not teaching them *what* a *text* wants them to say. Consequently, although each class begins with the same core vocabulary, the same illustrations and the same thematic questions, the final learned vocabulary, syntax, and cultural information will always vary.

**4.** Teachers of student-centered conversation classes often say (with delight!) that they learn from their students as they teach. ESL/EFL students learning a new language and culture are constantly confronted with cultural differences and communication problems. As a result, they frequently have a heightened awareness of their own values and of differences between their own cultural assumptions and expectations and those of the new culture. The sharing of individual perceptions of these differences (and similarities!) and strategies for coping with them make conversation classes a constant learning experience for those of us fortunate enough to teach them.

**5.** There are as many ways to use these materials as there are teachers and classes. Some teachers like the flexibility that the loose structure of the materials allows; others add the structure that fits their individual program design. Some test for vocabulary retention and conversation fluency; others do not. The chapters are not sequential and may be used in whatever order suits the class.

In revising the Conversation Books we have tried to be careful not to change what worked well in the first edition while updating the methodology, improving the design and eliminating outmoded exercises. Our goal is for students to develop a way to direct their own learning and feel comfortable in what they DO know so that from their conversation course, they can develop competencies and continue to learn and improve.

The good advice of many teachers and students over the years has helped us formulate this revision. We would like to extend our appreciation to them all, and our very *special* gratitude to two very *special* people: Christie Olson, without whom this revision would never have been started, and Ed Stanford, without whom it would never have been finished.

# All About You

1

# Welcome to Class!

## Questions for Conversation

*Practice asking and answering the questions with your teacher. Then ask your partner the questions.*

1.  What's* your name?          My name is _____

2.  Where are you from?          I'm** from _____
                                              (country)

3.  Where do you live            I live in _____
    now?                                      (city or town)

4.  What's* your
    **address?**                 My address is _____

5.  What is your **zip**          My zip code is _____
    code?

6.  What **language(s)** do
    you speak at home?           I speak _____

7.  Do you have a
    **telephone?**                (Yes)(No) _____

8.  What is your
    **telephone number?**         _____

*What's = What is    **I'm = I am

2

# Conversation Matrix: Icebreaker

1. *Write your name on Line 1.*
2. *Write your answers in the left column. (Answer the questions with I.)*
3. *Write your partner's name on Line 2.*
4. *Ask your partner the questions.*
5. *Write your partner's answers in the right column. (Answer the questions with He or She.)*
6. *Introduce yourself to the group, using the answers from the left column.*
7. *Introduce your partner to the group, using the answers from the right column.*

| | 1. _____ | 2. _____ |
|---|---|---|
| **a.** What's your name? | | |
| **b.** Where are you from? | | |
| **c.** Where do you live now? | | |
| **d.** What language(s) do you speak at home? | | |

# How Are You Today?

## With Your Partner

*Ask and answer with your partner.*

1. Are you **happy** today?
   Yes, I am.
   No, I'm not.

2. Are you **sad** today?
   Yes, I am.
   No, I'm not.

3. Are you **angry** today?
   Yes, I am.
   No, I'm not.

4. Are you **nervous** today?
   Yes, I am.
   No, I'm not.

5. Are you **tired** today?
   Yes, I am.
   No, I'm not.

6. Are you **sick** today?
   Yes, _____
   No, _____

7. Are you **hot** today?
   Yes, _____
   No, _____

8. Are you **cold** today?
   Yes, _____
   No, _____

9. Are you **hungry** today?
   Yes, _____
   No, _____

10. Are you **thirsty** today?
    Yes, _____
    No, _____

## Circle Dialogue

*Sit in a circle. Ask the student on your right the first question. ("Are you happy today?") That student answers and then asks the student on his or her right the same question.*

Teacher: "Are you happy today?"
Student 1: "Yes, I am." *or* "No, I'm not."
   "Are you happy today?"
Student 2: "Yes, I am. *or* "No, I'm not."
Continue around the circle. Repeat with all the questions on this page.

## List on the Board: What Do You Do?

*Ask the class these questions. Write a list on the board of all the different answers.*

1. What do you do when you are happy?
2. What do you do when you are sad?
3. What do you do when you are hot?
4. What do you do when you are tired?
5. What do you do when you are cold?
6. What do you do when you are angry?

# Who Is on Your Left?
# Who Is on Your Right?

## With Your Group

*Ask these questions in your group. (Use **He** and **His** for a man, **She** and **Her** for a woman.)*

1. Who is on your left? _____
2. How is he or she today? _____
3. Where is he or she from? _____
4. Who is on your right? _____
5. Where is he or she from? _____

## Find Someone Who

*Stand up and walk around the room. Ask your classmates these questions. Find out how everyone is today. Write the names of the students who say "yes."*

1. Are you nervous today? _____
2. Are you happy today? _____
3. Are you sad today? _____
4. Are you angry today? _____
5. Are you tired today? _____

# What Am I Doing?

*Fill in the blanks with the correct word. Read together. Then take turns demonstrating the actions.*

| closing | sitting | standing up |
|---------|---------|-------------|
| opening | walking | sitting down |
|         | standing |            |

He is _____ to the door.

He's* _____ the door.

He's _____ the door.

She is _____ to the window.

She's** _____ the window.

She's _____ the window.

She's _____ to her seat.

He is _____ .

Now he's _____ up.

He's _____ .

Now he's _____ down again.

He's _____ again.

*he's = he is  **she's = she is

*Fill in the blanks with the correct word. Then read together.*

| | | |
|---|---|---|
| listening | reading | coming |
| writing | talking | going |

She is _____ a book.

He is _____ a newspaper.

She is _____ a letter.

He is _____ a composition.

They are* _____ .

They are _____ to a tape.

She is _____ .

He is _____ .

Now he is _____ .

She is _____ .

She is _____ out of the room.

She is _____ into the room.

## List on the Board:
## What Do You Do in English Class?

*Make a list on the board of all the things you do in English class. Then choose one of the activities from the list. Demonstrate the action. Ask the class, "What am I doing?"*

## Demonstration Commands

*Take turns giving these commands and demonstrating the actions.*

1. Please stand up.
2. Please walk to the door.
3. Please open the door.
4. Please go out of the room.
5. Please come into the room.
6. Please close the door.

7. Please walk to the window.
8. Please open the window.
9. Please close the window.
10. Please walk to your seat.
11. Please sit down.
12. Please open a book.

13. Please read the book.
14. Please close the book.
15. Please write your name.

Thank you!

*They are = They're

**7**

# What Are You Wearing Today?

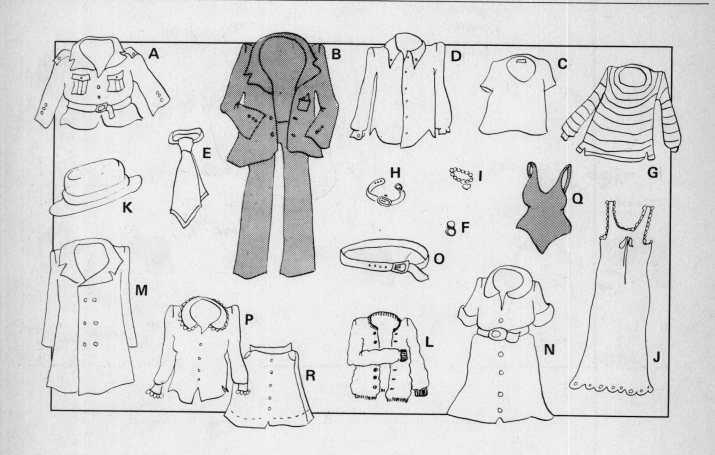

Practice this vocabulary with your teacher. Match the pictures with the words.

| | | | |
|---|---|---|---|
| a hat _____ | a nightgown _____ | a coat _____ | a blouse _____ |
| a suit _____ | a bracelet _____ | a T-shirt or _____ | a skirt _____ |
| a tie _____ | a jersey _____ | undershirt | a shirt _____ |
| a bathing suit _____ | a dress _____ | a jacket _____ | a watch _____ |
| a ring _____ | a belt _____ | sweater _____ | |

# Pairs of Clothing

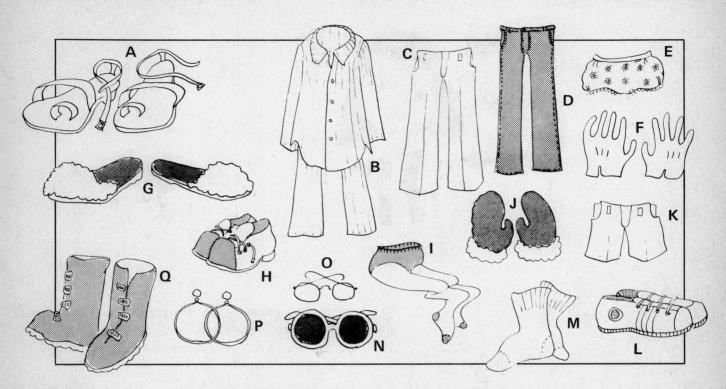

Practice this vocabulary with your teacher. Match the pictures with the words.

| | | |
|---|---|---|
| mittens _____ | sneakers _____ | stockings |
| slacks _____ | boots _____ | (pantyhose) _____ |
| socks _____ | pajamas _____ | underpants _____ |
| slippers _____ | shorts _____ | sandals _____ |
| jeans ___D_____ | shoes _____ | sunglasses _____ |
| gloves ___F_____ | glasses _____ | earrings _____ |

## With Your Partner

*Ask your partner about the pairs\* of clothing in the pictures.*

Student 1: "Are you wearing socks today?"
Student 2: "Yes, I am." *or* "No, I'm not."
     "Are you wearing earrings today?"
Student 1: "Yes, I am." *or* "No, I'm not."
     "Are you wearing _____ today?"

## Circle Dialogue

*Sit in a circle. Ask the student on the right, "What are you wearing today?" After he or she answers, he or she asks the next student, "What are you wearing today?" Continue around the circle.*

\*A pair of = two of the same   \*A pair of socks = two of the same sock

# What Color Are Your Clothes?

This woman is wearing a black and white striped jersey, white slacks, and black sandals.
What color are your clothes today?

## Circle Dialogue

*Do a circle dialogue with the question: "What color are your clothes today?"*

Teacher: "What color are your clothes today?"

Student 1: "My shoes are _____, my slacks are _____,
                  *(color)*                              *(color)*

     my shirt is _____. What color are your clothes today?"
                      *(color)*

Student 2: _____

*Continue around the circle.*

## With Your Partner

*Ask your partner, "What are you wearing today?" Then ask, "What color are your clothes?" Make a list. Report your answers to the class.*

# What Are They Wearing?

**With Your Class**

*Make a list on the board of the woman's clothing. Then make a list of the man's clothing.*

She's wearing

_____

_____

_____

_____

_____

_____

He's wearing

_____

_____

_____

_____

_____

_____

Discuss this picture with the class.
What is he saying?

## Conversation Matrix: Today

1. *Write your name on Line 1.*
2. *Write your answers in the left column. (Use I)*
3. *Write your partners' names on Lines 2 and 3.*
4. *Ask your partners the questions.*
5. *Write your answers in the other columns. (Use **He** or **She**.)*
6. *Report your answers to the group.*

| | 1. _____ | 2. _____ | 3. _____ |
|---|---|---|---|
| **a.** What are you wearing today? | | | |
| **b.** How are you today? | | | |
| **c.** What are you doing now? | | | |

# Lotto

**Lotto Word List**

nervous
sad
angry
tired
cold
hot
reading
writing
talking
walking
opening
closing
going
coming
standing
sitting
wearing
asking
answering
doing
feeling

**Lotto Instructions**

1. Copy any ten words from the LOTTO WORD LIST in the ten numbered boxes on your LOTTO SHEET.
2. Copy *the same ten words* in the bottom ten boxes on your LOTTO SHEET.
3. Tear out your LOTTO SHEET. Tear the *bottom* half into ten slips, with one word on each slip.
4. The teacher will call out the words on the WORD LIST, one at a time. When you have a word that the teacher calls, give the teacher your word slip. The teacher will make a pile of word slips for each word. (22 piles).
5. Exchange the top half of your LOTTO SHEET with another student.
6. The teacher will call out the words again, in a different order. If you have the word on your LOTTO SHEET, ask for a word slip. Put the word slip over the word on your LOTTO SHEET.
7. When you have a word slip for all ten words on your LOTTO SHEET, say: "LOTTO!" You win the game!

# Lotto Sheet

| | |
|---|---|
| 1. | 6. |
| 2. | 7. |
| 3. | 8. |
| 4. | 9. |
| 5. | 10. |

# 2

# About You
# and Your Family

# Parts of the Body

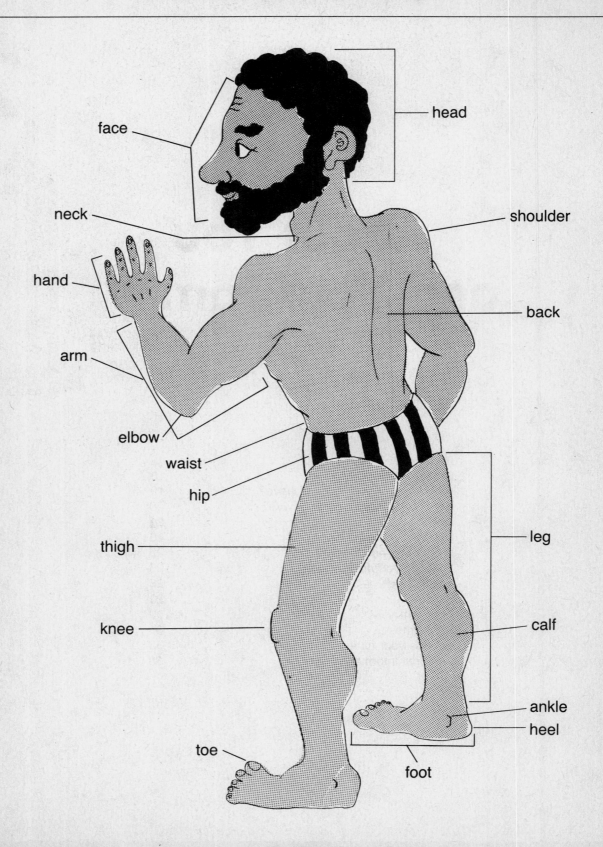

face

head

neck

shoulder

hand

back

arm

elbow

waist

hip

thigh

leg

knee

calf

ankle

heel

toe

foot

**16**

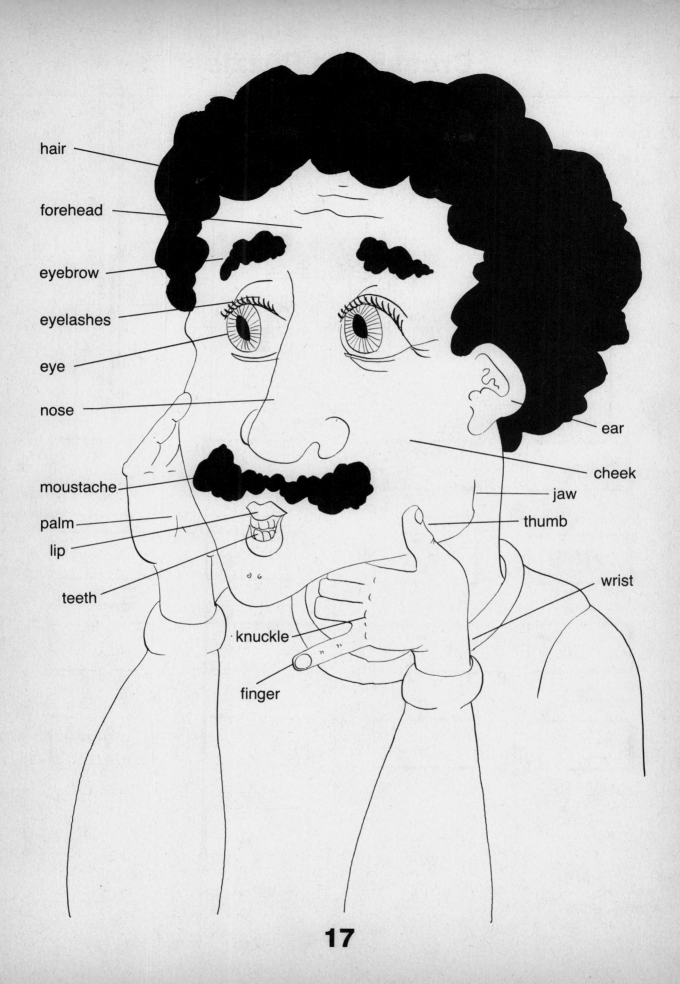

hair

forehead

eyebrow

eyelashes

eye

nose

moustache

palm

lip

teeth

ear

cheek

jaw

thumb

wrist

knuckle

finger

**17**

# Crossword Puzzle

Fill in this crossword puzzle.

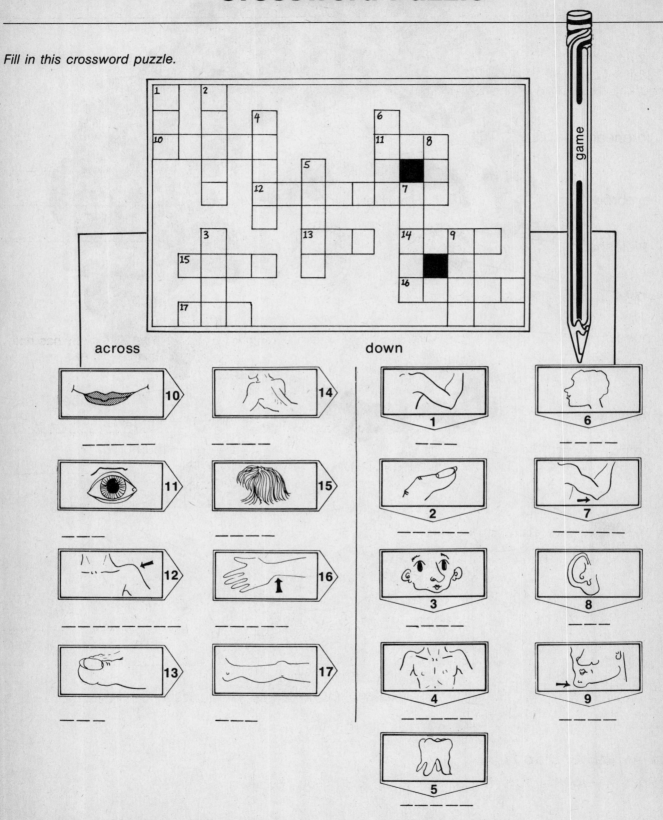

across

down

game

See answers on page 33

# How Many 👁 👁 Do You Have?

## With Your Class

*Answer These Questions with Complete Sentences*

1. How many **fingers**  do you have? I have _____

2. How many **thumbs**  do you have? _____

3. How many **feet**  do you have? _____

4. How many **toes**  do you have? _____

*Answer These Questions with Complete Sentences*

1. Does everybody have one **tongue**?  Yes, everybody has one tongue.

2. Does everybody have **fingernails**? _____

3. Does everybody have **teeth**?* _____

4. Does everybody have **hair**?** _____

*Answer These Questions with Short Answers*

1. Do you have a **moustache**? Yes, I do.
   OR No, I don't.

2. Do you have a **beard**? _____

3. Do you have **light hair**? _____

4. Do you have **dark hair**? _____

## Guessing Game: Who Is It?

*Describe a student for the class. The class must guess the student's name.*

*dentures  **bald

# How Much Money Do You Have?

## Money Circle Game

*Put some money on the table and ask a student to count it. Then add some money or take some away and ask another student to count it. Continue around the circle.*

## Picture Discussion

*This man has a problem. What is his problem? What should he do?*

## Role Play

*Pretend you are this man. Role-play asking a stranger for change.*

## Questions for Conversation

*With your group, take turns asking and answering these questions.*

1. Do you have any **cash** with you today?

2. How much cash do you have with you today?

3. Do you have any **change** with you today?

4. How much change do you have?

5. Do you have change for a dollar?

6. Do you have any **credit cards** with you today?

7. What credit cards do you have?

8. Do you have a **checkbook?** Which bank is it from?

9. How much is a dollar worth in your native country? (pesos, yen, cruzeiro, etc.)

# How Do We Tell Time?

It's nine o'clock.*
It's 9:00.

It's six-fifteen.**
It's 6:15.

It's five-twenty-five.**
It's 5:25.

It's three-thirty.**
It's 3:30.

It's one-forty-five.**
It's 1:45.

It's seven-fifty.**
It's 7:50.

## Different Clocks

*Write the correct name under these clocks. What time does each clock show?*

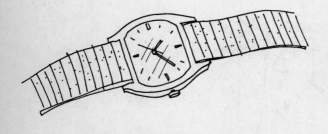

| |
|---|
| digital clock |
| grandfather clock |
| alarm clock |
| steeple clock |
| wristwatch |
| clock radio |

_____

_____

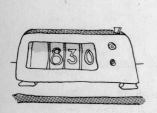

_____   _____   _____   _____

*It's = It is.

**What are some other ways of saying these times? Example: 6:15 can be a quarter past six or fifteen past six.

We also tell time like this:

5 to
10 to
quarter to
20 to
25 to

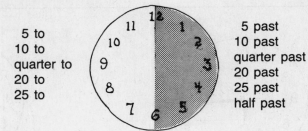

5 past
10 past
quarter past
20 past
25 past
half past

It's ten past four.

## What Time Is It?

It's five to three.

_____

_____

_____

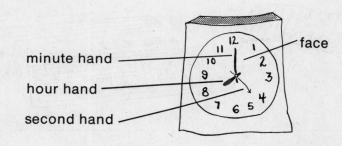

minute hand

hour hand

second hand

face

## Questions for Conversation

_Practice asking and answering these questions with your teacher. Then ask your partner the questions._

1. Are you wearing a watch?
2. Does it have a second hand?
3. What time is it?
4. Does this room have a clock?
5. Does it tell the same time as your watch?
6. What kind of clocks do you have at home?

22

# Daytime and Nighttime

## With Your Class

*Fill in the blanks. Then read together.*

| evening<br>daytime<br>at night<br>morning |

We are awake in the _____.

We sleep _____.

The sun rises in the _____

and sets in the _____.

| alarm clock<br>wake up<br>go to bed<br>get up |

When the _____ rings,

it is time to _____.

We _____ in the morning

and _____ at night.

| dinner<br>breakfast<br>supper<br>lunch |

We eat _____ in the morning.

We eat _____ at noon.

We eat _____ ( _____ ) in the evening.

| midnight<br>noon |

Twelve o'clock (12:00) at night is _____.

Twelve o'clock in the afternoon is _____.

23

## With Your Group

*Take turns asking and answering these questions. Fill in the times on the clocks.*

1. When does the sun rise? _____

2. When does the sun set? _____

3. Do you get up to watch the sun rise? _____

4. What time do you usually get up? _____

5. What time do you usually go to bed? _____

6. Do you work days or nights? _____

7. What time does your work start? _____

8. What time does this class start? _____

9. What time do you usually eat lunch? _____

10. What time do you usually eat supper?* _____

*__Supper__ and __dinner__ have different meanings in some places. What do these words mean where you live?

**24**

# What Does He Do Every Morning?

*Read this with your class.*

Every morning when the alarm clock **rings**  he **wakes**

**up.**  He **yawns,**  **stretches,**

and **gets out of bed.**  He **washes his face,**

**brushes his teeth,**  and **shaves.**

He **takes off** his pajamas,  **puts on** his clothes,

and **combs** his hair.  He **goes to** the kitchen,

**drinks** a cup of coffee,  **eats** breakfast,

and **goes** to work.

## With Your Partner

*What do you do every morning? Tell your partner. (Use **I**.)*

# What Do You Do Every Day?

## Do You Work?

*Fill in the blanks and the clocks in the paragraphs below.*

I work at _____. It is in _____.
(name of company or place)                        (city or town)

I'm a _____. My job is _____.
(name of your job)                        (what you do)

Every morning, I leave my house at _____. I work until

_____. I get home at _____. I have dinner at

_____. I watch television or listen to the radio after

dinner. I go to bed at _____.

## Do You Work at Home?

I work at home. When the alarm clock rings at _____

_____, I get up. I prepare _____ in the kitchen. I get
(name of meal)

dressed at _____. Before lunch, I _____.
(what do you do before lunch?)

I eat lunch at _____. In the afternoon, I _____.
(what do you do in the afternoon?)

I prepare dinner at _____. I eat dinner at _____.

After dinner, I _____. I go to bed at
(what do you do after dinner?)

_____.

26

*your bones = los os*

*Take a bath*
*shower*

## Conversation Matrix: Daily Routine

1. *Write your name on Line 1.*
2. *Write your answers in the left column.*
3. *Write your partners' names on Lines 2 and 3.*
4. *Ask your partners the questions.*
5. *Write your partners' answers in the other columns.*
6. *Report your answers to the group.*

*(nu-)*
*costumed Adam = naked*

| | 1. _____ | 2. _____ | 3. _____ |
|---|---|---|---|
| **a.** What time do you get up in the morning? | | | |
| **b.** What do you do every day? | | | |
| **c.** Where do you eat lunch? | | | |
| **d.** When do you go to bed at night? | | | |

*To believe*
*belief*
*bel*

*I dress up*
*I put on my clothes*
*I catch the bus*
*and I go to school!*
*incredule — unbeliever or non*
*u*

**27**

# Family Tree

JOE JANE

BILL

NANCY

MARY

# Families

## Vocabulary

| Male | Female | Both Sexes |
|------|--------|------------|
| husband | wife | spouse |
| father | mother | parent |
| brother | sister | sibling |
| son | daughter | child |
| grandson | granddaughter | grandchild |
| uncle | aunt | — |
| nephew | niece | — |
| — | — | cousin |
| divorcé | divorcée | — |
| widower | widow | — |
| father-in-law | mother-in-law | in-law |
| son-in-law | daughter-in-law | — |
| brother-in-law | sister-in-law | — |
| man (men) | woman (women) | adult |
| boy | girl | child (children) |
| | | baby (babies) |
| | | adolescent |
| | | teenager |
| | | youth |
| | | young person (young people) |

## Questions

1. Which people in the picture are grandparents?
2. Which people are parents?
3. Which people are children?
4. How many uncles are there in the picture? How many aunts?
5. How many parents are there?
6. Who are in-laws?
7. Are the children cousins?
8. Which people are daughters? Sons? Brothers? Siblings?
9. Which people are men? Boys? Women? Girls?
10. How many **generations** do you see?

## Your Family Tree

Using the family tree in the book, construct your own family tree by putting the names of your family members under each person. Draw extra people if your family has more members. Put an X through the people you do not need for your family tree. OR on a separate piece of paper, draw your own family tree.

# Your Family

## With Your Partner

*Practice asking and answering the questions with your teacher. Then ask your partner the questions.*

**1.** Are you married?

**2.** What is your wife's (husband's) name?

**3.** Do you have any children?

**4.** How many children do you have?

**5.** What is your child's name? (What are your children's names?)

**6.** How old is your child? (How old are your children?)

**7.** Do you have any brothers and sisters?

**8.** How many brothers and sisters do you have?

**9.** How old are your brothers and sisters?

**10.** Do you have any nephews or nieces?

**11.** Are your parents living?

**12.** Where does your family live?

**13.** Do you live with your family?

## Class Activity

*Do you have photographs of your family? Bring them to class and show them to your classmates.*

# Nicknames

Many Americans have **nicknames**. A **nickname** is a name that people call you instead of your legal first name. Often nicknames are short names. Many children's nicknames end in **-y** in English. Do you know the nicknames for these names?

| Given name | Child's nickname | Adult's nickname |
|---|---|---|
| Edward | | |
| Elizabeth | | |
| James | | |
| John | | |
| Joseph | | |
| Katherine | | |
| Margaret | | |
| Patricia | | |
| Peter | | |
| Robert | | |
| Susan | | |
| Thomas | | |
| William | | |
| | | |
| | | |

## Questions for Conversation

1. Which of these nicknames are for girls and women? Which are for boys and men?
2. Do you have a nickname? What is it?
3. The names on this list are all very common first names (given names) in English. What are some common first names in your native language?
4. Some common family names* in English are Brown, Johnson, Jones, Smith, and White. What are some common family names in your native language?
5. In the United States there are many different kinds of family names because Americans come from so many different countries. In your native country do many family names have the same ending? (For example: In Armenia, family names end in *-ian*.)

*last name

# What Is Your Nationality?

People from many countries live in the United States because it is a nation of immigrants. Here are the names of some of the **nations** people come from and their **nationalities.** Notice that many nationalities end in **-ese, -ish,** or **-an.** Can you fill in the blanks in each list with more nations and nationalities?

| Nation | Nationality | Nation | Nationality |
|--------|-------------|--------|-------------|
| Burma | Burmese | Denmark | Danish |
| China | Chinese | England | English |
| Japan | Japanese | Ireland | Irish |
| Lebanon | Lebanese | Poland | Polish |
| Portugal | Portuguese | Sweden | Swedish |
| Vietnam | Vietnamese | Turkey | Turkish |
| \_\_\_\_\_ | \_\_\_\_\_ | \_\_\_\_\_ | \_\_\_\_\_ |
| Armenia | Armenian | Chile | Chilean |
| Brazil | Brazilian | Cuba | Cuban |
| Canada | Canadian | The Dominican Republic | Dominican |
| Colombia | Colombian | Germany | German |
| Ecuador | Ecuadorian | Kenya | Kenyan |
| Egypt | Egyptian | Korea | Korean |
| Ethiopia | Ethiopian | Mexico | Mexican |
| Hungary | Hungarian | Puerto Rico* | Puerto Rican |
| India | Indian | Uganda | Ugandan |
| Indonesia | Indonesian | The United States of America (U.S.A.) | American |
| Iran | Iranian | | |
| Italy | Italian | | |
| Panama | Panamanian | Venezuela | Venezuelan |
| Russia (USSR) | Russian | | |
| Tahiti | Tahitian | | |
| \_\_\_\_\_ | \_\_\_\_\_ | \_\_\_\_\_ | \_\_\_\_\_ |
| \_\_\_\_\_ | \_\_\_\_\_ | \_\_\_\_\_ | \_\_\_\_\_ |

What is your nationality?

What nation are you from?

Note: See **Appendix** for maps.

*Puerto Rico is a commonwealth; its citizens are citizens of the United States.

# Personal Information Form

*Fill in this personal information form:*

1. What is your name?
   _____

2. What is your address?
   _____

3. Height: _____ Weight: _____
   Color of Eyes: _____ Color of Hair: _____

4. What are you wearing today?
   _____

5. What colors are your clothes?
   _____

6. How much money do you have with you?
   _____

7. How are you feeling today?
   _____

8. What are you doing now?
   _____

9. What is the teacher doing now?
   _____

10. Are you married?
    _____

11. Are your parents living?
    _____

12. Do you have any children? _____
    How many? _____ How old? _____
    Sons? _____ Daughters? _____

13. Do you have any sisters? _____
    Brothers? _____
    How many? _____ How old? _____

## Crossword Puzzle Solution

**Across:** 10. mouth   11. eye   12. shoulder   13. toe
14. back   15. hair   16. wrist   17. leg

**Down:** 1. arm   2. thumb   3. face   4. chest   3. tooth
6. head   7. elbow   8. ear   9. chin

# Homes

**3**

# Where Do You Live?

## Vocabulary

*Repeat the vocabulary with your teacher. Write the name of each place below the picture.*

| ranch | farm | town | military base | beach |
|---|---|---|---|---|
| desert | city | mountains | country | |

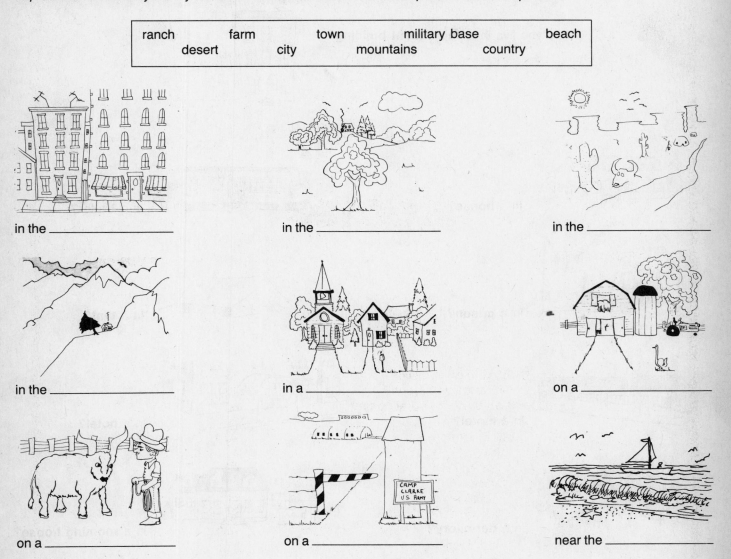

in the _____

in the _____

in the _____

in the _____

in a _____

on a _____

on a _____

on a _____

near the _____

## Interview Questions

*Practice asking and answering these questions with your teacher. Then ask your partner the questions. Finally, present your interview to the class.*

1. Where do you live now? Is it a city? Is it a town? Is it in the mountains? Is it in the desert?
2. What street do you live on? What is your address?
3. Where were you born? In the city or in the country?
4. Which do you prefer—the city or the country? Why?
5. Which do you prefer—the mountains, the desert, or the beach? Why?

# What Do You Live In?

Read with your class and answer the questions.*

Do you live in an **apartment building?**

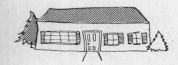 In a **house?**

 In a **trailer?**

 In a **prison?**

 In a **tent?**

 In a **motel?**

 In a **hotel?**

 In a **dormitory?**

 In a **rooming house?**

## With Your Class

Read and answer the questions.

1. What is your address?
2. What do you live in?
3. What would you like to live in?
4. What state in the United States would you like to live in? Why?

*See **Appendix,** Map of the United States.

# What Do You Do At Home?

## Find Someone Who

*Stand up and walk around the classroom. Talk to your classmates. Find someone who does each of these things at home. Write the students' names.*

*Ex: (Ask, "Do you eat lunch at home?")*

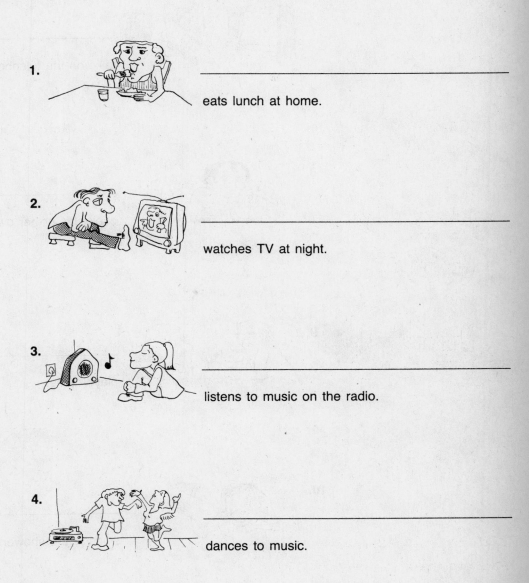

1. _____

   eats lunch at home.

2. _____

   watches TV at night.

3. _____

   listens to music on the radio.

4. _____

   dances to music.

5. _____

   reads books.

**37**

**6.**

_____
writes letters.

**7.**

_____
talks on the telephone.

**8.**

_____
cooks his or her own meals.

**9.**

_____
plays cards.

**10.**

_____
sings in the shower.

**11.**

_____
sleeps well every night.

# Bedroom

*Read this vocabulary with your teacher. Practice it with a partner.*

| | | | |
|---|---|---|---|
| **1.** bed | **6.** bedspread | **11.** chest of drawers | **16.** rug |
| **2.** pillow | **7.** bedside table | **12.** drawer | **17.** closet |
| **3.** pillowcase | **8.** lamp | **13.** comb | **18.** window |
| **4.** sheets | **9.** lampshade | **14.** brush | **19.** curtains |
| **5.** blanket | **10.** dresser | **15.** mirror | **20.** shade |

*Fill in the blanks and read the sentences with your class.*

**1.** When you make a bed, you put on a _____, two _____, and a _____ . You put a _____ on the pillow.

**2.** On this window, there is a _____ and _____. At night, you pull down the _____.

**3.** You hang your clothes in the _____. You fold other clothes and put them in the _____ or the _____.

**4.** At night, you climb into _____, cover up with the _____ and _____, switch off the _____, lay your head on the _____, and go to sleep. Sweet dreams!

## Class Discussion: Bedrooms in Your Native Country

*Are bedrooms in your native country different from this picture? Describe them to the class.*

## With Your Partner: Childhood Memory

*Where did you sleep when you were a child? Describe it to your partner.*

# Bathroom

*Practice this vocabulary with your teacher.*

| | | |
|---|---|---|
| 1. bathtub | 6. soap | 11. washcloth |
| 2. drain | 7. tiles | 12. sink |
| 3. shower | 8. rug | 13. mirror |
| 4. faucet | 9. wastebasket | 14. toilet |
| 5. shower curtain | 10. towel | 15. toilet paper |

*Fill in the blanks as your teacher reads the paragraph.*

In the bathroom, you can wash your face at the _____ with _____ and water and dry it with a _____. You can take a _____ or a _____ in the _____. Don't forget to pull the plug so the water can go down the _____.

## Class Discussion: Bathrooms in Your Native Country

*Are bathrooms in your native country different from this picture? Describe them for the class.*

# Living Room

*Practice this vocabulary with your teacher.*

| | | |
|---|---|---|
| **1.** sofa | **5.** lamp | **10.** fireplace |
| **2.** armchair | **6.** ashtray | **11.** picture |
| **3.** end table | **7.** plant | **12.** draperies |
| **4.** cocktail table | **8.** television | **13.** carpet |
| | **9.** stereo | |

*Fill in the blanks as your teacher reads the sentences.*

1. When you watch _____ or listen to the _____ in this living room you can sit in the _____ or on the _____ .

2. In this living room, there are _____ on the windows. There is a _____ on the wall. There is a _____ on the floor. On the tables, there is a _____, a _____, and a _____ .

## Pantomime Game: Living Room Activities

*Make a list on the board of things you can do in the living room. Take turns pantomiming activities from the list for the class to guess.*

# Dining Area

*Practice this vocabulary with your teacher.*

1. dining table
2. tablecloth
3. chairs
4. candles
5. plates
6. silverware:
   a. knife
   b. fork
   c. spoon
7. napkins
8. water glass
9. wine glass
10. buffet
11. fruit bowl

## Questions for Conversation

1. How do you set the table at your home for breakfast?
2. How do you set it for lunch?
3. How do you set it for supper?
4. In your native country, do people eat meals at a table?
5. Do they sit on chairs?
6. Please tell the class how people eat meals in your native country. Is it the same as in the United States?

# Kitchen

Match the words on the list with the numbers in the picture.

|  |  |  |  |
|---|---|---|---|
| _____ refrigerator | _____ stove | _____ lid (cover) | _____ linoleum |
| _____ sink | _____ oven | _____ cabinet | _____ cup |
| _____ faucet | _____ burner | _____ cupboard | _____ saucer |
| _____ dishpan | _____ tea kettle | _____ counter | _____ coffee pot |
| _____ dishwasher | _____ pot | _____ toaster | _____ dish |
| _____ washing machine | _____ frying pan | _____ electric mixer | _____ sugar bowl |
| _____ dryer |  | _____ can opener |  |

## Questions for Conversation

1. In your native country, do people shop for food every day? Once a week? How often?
2. Do you use canned foods? What kinds?
3. Do you use frozen foods? What kinds? Do you know how to freeze food from the supermarket?
4. Do you have appliances in your kitchen? What appliances do you like? What other appliances would you like to have?
5. What are kitchens like in your native country?

43

# Inside Your Home

## Vocabulary Review

*Look at this picture with a partner and see how many vocabulary words you can remember.*

## With Your Partner

*Practice asking and answering these questions with your teacher. Then ask your partner the questions.*

1. What room do you sleep in?
2. What room do you take a bath or shower in?
3. Where do you eat?
4. Where do you study?
5. Where do you sit and talk?
6. Where do you watch TV?
7. Where do you cook?

# Your Neighborhood

## Questions for Conversation

1. Do you like your neighborhood? How long have you lived there?
2. Is it very different from your neighborhood in your native country or city? What is different?

## Neighborhood Map

*Draw a map of your neighborhood. Show buildings, mailboxes, fire boxes, parks, and street names. Explain your map to the other students.*

## With Your Partner

*Practice asking and answering these questions with your teacher. Then ask your partner the questions. Report your interview to the class.*

1. Do you live near a highway?
2. Do you live near a park?
3. Do you live near a shopping center?
4. Do you live near a playground?
5. Do you live far from the mountains?
6. Do you live far from the ocean?
7. Do you live far from an airport?
8. Do you live far from a hospital?
9. How far do you live from work?
10. How far do you live from school?
11. How far do you live from a mailbox?
12. How far do you live from a bus stop?

# Your Neighbors

## With Your Partner

*Practice asking and answering these questions with your teacher. Then ask your partner the questions.*

1. Do you know any of your neighbors? How long have you known them?
2. Are your neighbors friendly? Do you ever visit them?
3. Do your neighbors speak English? Do they speak any other languages?
4. Do the children in your neighborhood play together? Do they ever fight? What games do they play?
5. Do you know your next-door neighbors well? What are their names? Tell the class about them.
6. Do you ever have any problems with any of your neighbors? Tell the class about them.

## Problems for Discussion

*The pictures below show problems between neighbors. What is happening in each picture? Did you ever have any of these problems with your neighbors? Tell the class about them.*

Children Fighting

Noisy Parties

Gossip

## Role Play

*With a group of students, choose one of these three problems to role play. Practice your role play and present it to your class.*

# Housecleaning

What are they doing?

*Fill in the blanks. Then read together.*

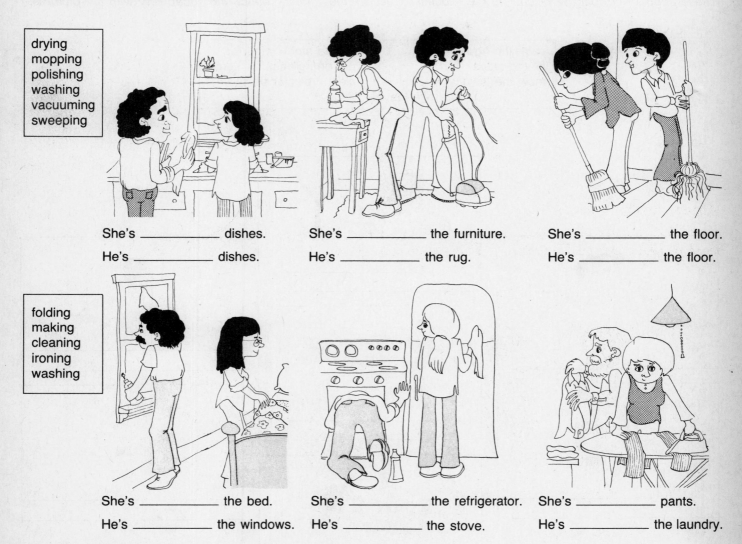

| drying |
| mopping |
| polishing |
| washing |
| vacuuming |
| sweeping |

She's _____ dishes.

He's _____ dishes.

She's _____ the furniture.

He's _____ the rug.

She's _____ the floor.

He's _____ the floor.

| folding |
| making |
| cleaning |
| ironing |
| washing |

She's _____ the bed.

He's _____ the windows.

She's _____ the refrigerator.

He's _____ the stove.

She's _____ pants.

He's _____ the laundry.

## Questions for Discussion

*Answer these questions and discuss them with your group.*

1. Who does the housecleaning in your home?
2. In your native country, do men help with the housecleaning?
3. Should men ever help with the housecleaning? Why or why not?
4. In some countries, housewives wash the sidewalks and steps outside their houses every day. In the United States, they do not. Are there any differences like this between housecleaning in your native country and the United States?

# Work Outside the House

## Vocabulary

*These people are doing work outside their houses. What are they doing? Match the vocabulary with the pictures.*

| | |
|---|---|
| paint the house | put up storm windows |
| fix the steps | put on screens for summer |
| mow the lawn | clean up after pets |
| | rake leaves |

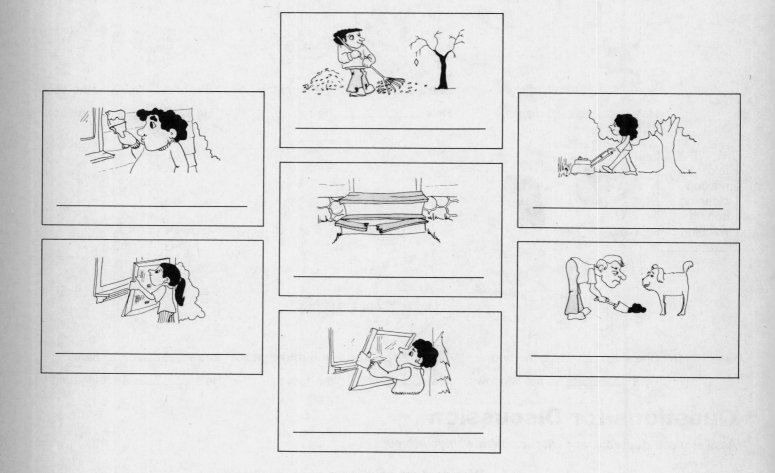

## Questions for Conversation

1. In the country, what work do you do outside? In the city? In the suburbs?
2. Is there more work outside the house in the country, the suburbs, or the city?
3. Where do you prefer to work, outside the house or inside? Why?

# Gardening

## Vocabulary

*This woman is gardening. What is she doing? Match the vocabulary with the appropriate picture.*

| | |
|---|---|
| water the garden | plant the seeds |
| till the ground | weed the garden |

_____

_____

_____

_____

## Questions for Conversation

1. Did you ever have a vegetable garden?
2. What vegetables did you grow?
3. Did you ever have a flower garden?
4. What flowers did you grow?
5. What are your favorite flowers?
6. When is the growing season in your native country or city?

# City Animals/Farm Animals

**Vocabulary:**
**Farm Animals**

*Match the words on the list with the animals in the picture.*

| | | | | |
|---|---|---|---|---|
| ___ horse | ___ sheep* | ___ rooster | ___ bull | ___ goose** |
| ___ colt | ___ lamb | ___ hen | ___ cow | ___ gosling |
| ___ duck | ___ dog | ___ chick | ___ calf | ___ pig |
| ___ duckling | ___ puppy | | | |

## Questions for Conversation

1. Have you ever raised any of these animals? Which ones?
2. Which domesticated animals does a farmer raise to eat?
3. What else do we use these farm animals for? (Cows give milk, etc.)
4. What animals do farmers raise in your native country?

*The plural of sheep is sheep.      **The plural of goose is geese.

## Vocabulary:
## City Animals

*Match the words on the list with the animals in the picture.*

| | | | | |
|---|---|---|---|---|
| ___ rat | ___ pigeon | ___ dog | ___ fish** | ___ cat |
| ___ bird | ___ guinea pig | ___ mouse* | | |

## Questions for Conversation

1. What animals do people usually have for pets in your native country?
2. Does your city have a leash law?
3. Are there any stray animals in this picture?
4. Are mice and rats domesticated animals?
5. What noises do all these animals make in your native language? In English?

*The plural of mouse is mice.    **The plural of fish is fish.

# Home Repairs

## List on the Board

*What home repairs can you do with these tools? Make a list.*

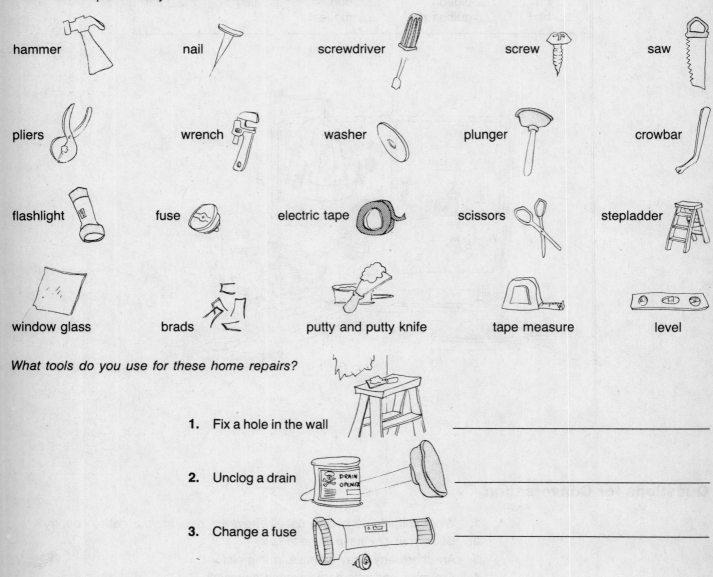

| | | | | |
|---|---|---|---|---|
| hammer | nail | screwdriver | screw | saw |
| pliers | wrench | washer | plunger | crowbar |
| flashlight | fuse | electric tape | scissors | stepladder |
| window glass | brads | putty and putty knife | tape measure | level |

*What tools do you use for these home repairs?*

1.  Fix a hole in the wall  _____

2.  Unclog a drain  _____

3.  Change a fuse  _____

## Problems for Discussion

1.  What should you do if your roof leaks?
2.  What should you do if you have no hot water?
3.  What should you do it you smell gas in your apartment?
4.  What should you do if your refrigerator doesn't work?
5.  What should you do if you drop a gold ring down the sink drain?
6.  What should you do if all the lights go out?
7.  What should you do if you break a window at home?

# Insurance

## Problems for Discussion

*What is happening in these pictures? How can insurance help in these situations?*

## Questions for Conversation

*Practice asking and answering these questions with your teacher. Then ask your partner the questions.*

1. Do you have any insurance? What kind of insurance do you have?
2. Did you ever collect from your insurance? What happened?
3. Do people in your native country carry insurance? What kind?

## Role Playing

*With your group, choose one of these picture problems to role play. Practice your role play and present it for the class.*

# Days, Dates, and Weather

**4**

# Days and Dates

## With Your Class

*Practice saying the **days*** of the week:*

Sunday (Sun.)**
Monday (Mon.)
Tuesday (Tues.)
Wednesday (Wed.)
Thursday (Thurs.)
Friday (Fri.)
Saturday (Sat.)

What day is **today?**_____

What day was **yesterday**?_____

What day will **tomorrow** be?_____

*Practice saying the **months*** of the year:*

January (Jan.)
February (Feb.)
March (Mar.)
April (Apr.)
May
June (Jun.)
July (Jul.)
August (Aug.)
September (Sept.)
October (Oct.)
November (Nov.)
December (Dec.)

What is the **month** now?_____

What was last month?_____

What will next month be?_____

*Practice saying these **years**. Do you know why these years are important in the United States?****

1492 (fourteen ninety-two)
1620 (sixteen twenty)
1776 (seventeen seventy-six)

What is the **year** now?_____

What was last year?_____

What will next year be?_____

## With Your Class: Vocabulary Review

1. How many days are there in a **weekend**?
2. How many weeks are there in a **year**?
3. How many months are there in a **year**?
4. How many years are there in a **century**?
5. How many days are there in each **month**?
6. How many days are there in a **leap year**?
7. What will the date be the day after **tomorrow**?
8. What day was the day before **yesterday**?

*Days and months in parentheses (  ) are abbreviations (short forms).
**Another way to abbreviate the names of the days of the week: M, T, W, Th, F, (Sa, Su. not used often).
***See answer on pg. **68**

## With Your Partner

*Practice asking and answering these questions with your teacher. Then ask your partner the questions. Finally, report your interview to the class.*

1. When is your birthday?
2. What year were you born?
3. What is your favorite day of the week? Why?
4. What is your favorite month? Why?

## Picture for Conversation: Birthday Party

*What is happening in this picture? Do people celebrate birthdays in your native country? How?*

| presents |
| --- |
| candles |
| decorations |
| balloons |
| crepe paper |
| blindfold |
| Pin-the-tail |
| -on-the-donkey |

## Class Discussion: Different Calendars

Most countries in the Western world use the Gregorian calendar. However, some parts of the world use different calendars. When is the new year celebrated in your native country? If you know about a different calendar, tell the class about it.

# Crossword Puzzle

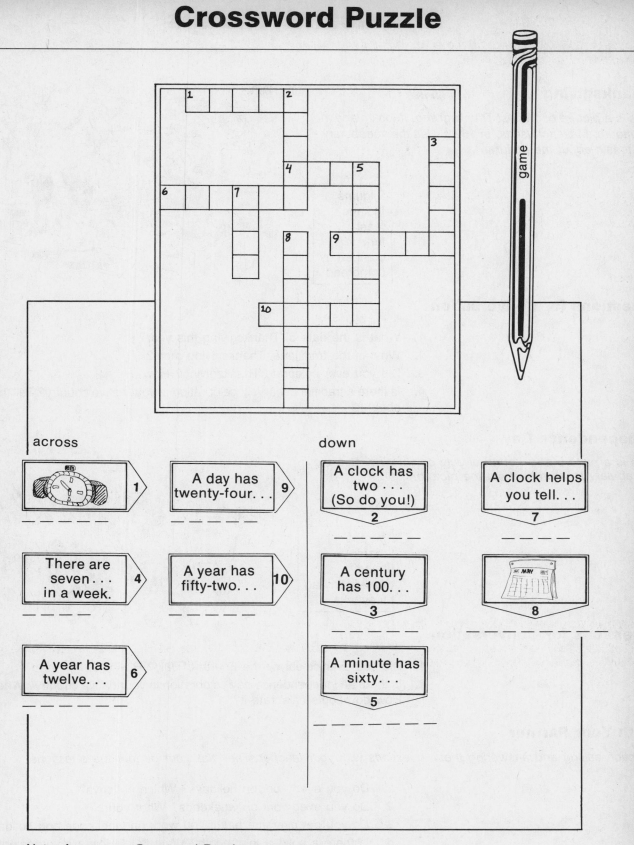

across

1

9 A day has twenty-four...

4 There are seven... in a week.

10 A year has fifty-two...

6 A year has twelve...

down

2 A clock has two... (So do you!)

3 A century has 100...

5 A minute has sixty...

7 A clock helps you tell...

8

Note: Answers to Crossword Puzzle on page 68

# American Holidays

## Thanksgiving

*This is a picture of the first Thanksgiving. It took place in Plymouth, Massachusetts, in 1621. Use the vocabulary list to talk about the picture.*

Pilgrims
Indians
feast
turkey
cranberries
cornbread

## Questions for Conversation

1. What is the date of Thanksgiving this year?
2. What is the traditional Thanksgiving meal?
3. Did you ever celebrate Thanksgiving? How?
4. Is there a traditional harvest celebration in your native country? Tell the class about it.

## Independence Day

*This is a picture of a Fourth of July celebration. Use the vocabulary list to talk about the picture.*

parade
march
band
American flag
fireworks

## Questions for Conversation

1. Did you ever celebrate the Fourth of July? How?
2. Is there an independence day celebration in your native country? When is it? How do people celebrate it?

## With Your Partner

*Practice asking and answering these questions with your teacher. Then ask your partner the questions.*

1. Do you ever work on holidays? Which holidays?
2. Do you ever work on weekends? What hours?
3. Do you get overtime pay if you work on weekends and holidays?
4. Is there a holiday this month? What is it? How will you celebrate it?
5. What is your favorite holiday? Why? How do you celebrate it?

# Holidays

## Vocabulary

*Practice this vocabulary with your teacher. Fill in the blanks. Then read the sentences together and discuss the holiday pictures.*

| | | |
|---|---|---|
| party horns | corsage | ghost |
| Valentine candy | wreath | witch |
| Easter bunny | flag | jack-o'-lanterns |
| Christmas tree | turkey | Easter eggs |
| | barbeques | |

New Year's Eve

At New Year's Eve parties, people blow p _ _ _ _ h _ _ _ _ _ at midnight.

Independence Day

On the Fourth of July, people watch fireworks and fly American f _ _ _ _ .

St. Valentine's Day

On St. Valentine's Day, people give valentines and V _ _ _ _ _ _ _ _ _ c _ _ _ _ _ .

Labor Day

On Labor Day, many people have b _ _ _ _ _ _ _ _ _ in their back yards.

Halloween

On Halloween, children dress up as g _ _ _ _ _ and w _ _ _ _ _ _, and make j _ _ _ _ _ _ _ _ _ _ _ _ _ _ out of pumpkins.

Easter

On Easter, children hunt for E _ _ _ _ _ e _ _ _ left by the E _ _ _ _ _ b _ _ _ _ .

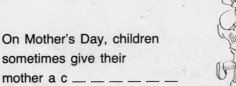

Thanksgiving

On Thanksgiving, people eat t _ _ _ _ _ _ and watch football games.

Mother's Day

On Mother's Day, children sometimes give their mother a c _ _ _ _ _ _ of flowers.

Christmas

On Christmas, people decorate C _ _ _ _ _ _ _ _ t _ _ _ _ , give presents, and send Christmas cards.

Memorial Day

On Memorial Day, people put w _ _ _ _ _ _ of flowers on graves to remember the dead.

See answers, p.68

**59**

# Christmas in the United States

## Matching

*Match these pictures with the activities:*

1. baking Christmas cookies and fruitcakes
2. Christmas pageants
3. decorating the tree
4. Christmas shopping
5. sending Christmas cards and gifts
6. opening Christmas gifts

## Questions for Conversation

1. Do you celebrate Christmas?
2. Do you have a Christmas tree at Christmas? What do you decorate it with?
3. Do you give Christmas presents? To whom?
4. Do you eat any special food at Christmastime? What food?
5. In the United States, Christmas is both a religious holiday for Christians and a national holiday for everyone. In your native country, is there any holiday that is both a religious and a national holiday? Tell about it.
6. Christmas is the biggest holiday in the United States. What is the biggest holiday in your native country? How do people celebrate it?

Note: See **Appendix** for "Jingle Bells."

# Weather

## Pictures for Conversation

*Answer the questions about these pictures, using the vocabulary lists.*

| clouds | grass |
|--------|-------|
| flowers | sun |
| trees | shine |
| hill | |

1. Describe the weather in this picture.
2. What is the man doing?
3. Did you ever lie out in the sun? Tell about it.

dust storm
cactus
wind
blow
sand

1. Describe the weather in this picture.
2. What are the man and the horse doing?
3. Were you ever out in a dust storm? What did you do?

leaves
branches
pile
rake
bare
cool
cloudy

1. Describe the weather in this picture.
2. What is the man doing?
3. Did you ever rake leaves? What did you do with the leaves after you raked them?

skis
ski poles
ski boots
fall down
ski slope
cold
sunny

1. Describe the weather in this picture.
2. What are the people doing?
3. Did you ever go skiing? Where?

**61**

umbrella
raincoat
rainy
raining
wet
wait
curb
poncho

1. Describe the weather in this picture.
2. What are the people wearing?
3. What are they doing?
4. Were you ever caught in the rain? What did you do?

snowy
snowing
snow shovel
snowflakes
snowdrift

1. Describe the weather in this picture.
2. What are the people wearing?
3. What are they doing?
4. Were you ever out in a snowstorm? What did you do?

hailing
hailstones
picnic table
picnic basket
bench

1. Describe the weather in this picture.
2. What are the people doing?
3. Were you ever out in a hailstorm? What did you do?

thunderstorm
thunder
lightning
bolt
storm cloud

1. Describe the weather in this picture.
2. What is the girl doing?
3. Were you ever out in a thunderstorm? What did you do?

**62**

# Seasonal Clothing

## Vocabulary

*Practice this vocabulary with your teacher.*

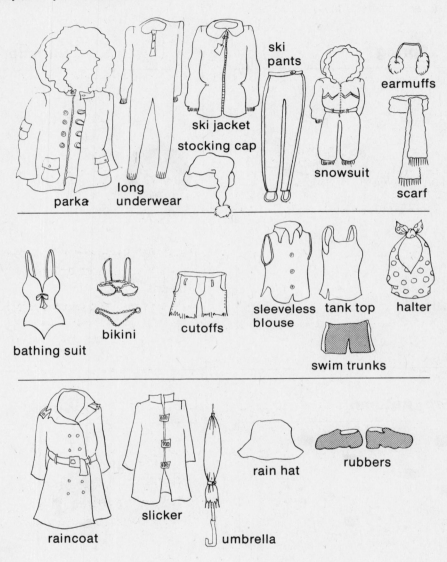

parka · long underwear · ski jacket · stocking cap · ski pants · snowsuit · earmuffs · scarf

bathing suit · bikini · cutoffs · sleeveless blouse · tank top · halter · swim trunks

raincoat · slicker · umbrella · rain hat · rubbers

## With Your Partner

*Practice asking and answering these questions with your teacher. Then ask your partner the questions. Finally, present your interview to the class.*

1. What do you wear in cold weather?
2. What do you wear when it rains?
3. What do you wear in hot weather?
4. Do people in your country wear any of this seasonal clothing? Do they have other special clothing? Tell about it.

# Seasons

## Pictures for Discussion

*Are the four seasons the same in your native country as in the United States? What are the people doing in these pictures? Did you ever do any of these things?*

### Spring

### Summer

### Fall (Autumn)

### Winter

# Seasonal Activities

## Pictures for Conversation

*Use the vocabulary lists to talk about the pictures with your partner.*

| | | |
|---|---|---|
| sunglasses | sand | ocean |
| bathing suit | beach | radio |
| umbrella | pail | shovel |
| shoreline | bikini | |

1. What season is this?
2. What are the people wearing?
3. Where are they?
4. What are they doing?

| | | |
|---|---|---|
| snowplow | snowman | coal |
| snowbank | snowball | plow |

1. What season is this?
2. What are the people wearing?
3. What are they doing?

| | |
|---|---|
| lunch box | dead leaves |
| schoolbooks | school bus |
| sidewalk | bicycle |

1. What season is this?
2. What are the people wearing?
3. Where are the children going?
4. What is the man doing?

## Role Play: Talking about the Weather

*Choose one of these situations to act out with your partner for the class.*

1. Two people riding in a car in a blizzard.
2. Two people on a picnic when it starts hailing.
3. Two people at the beach when a thunderstorm is coming.
4. Two people waiting at the bus stop in the rain.
5. Two students sitting in class talking about the weather today.

## With Your Partner

*Practice asking and answering these questions with your teacher. Then ask your partner the questons. Report your interview to the class.*

1. When it is very hot, how do you stay cool?
2. When it is cold, how do you stay warm?
3. Which is your favorite season? Why?
4. Which season do you like the least? Why?

## Conversation Matrix: What Is Your Favorite?

1. *Write your name on Line 1.*
2. *Write your answers in the left column. (Use **I**).*
3. *Write your partners' names on Lines 2 and 3.*
4. *Ask your partners the questions.*
5. *Write your answers in the other columns. (Use **He** or **She**.)*
6. *Report your answers to the group.*

| | 1. _____ | 2. _____ | 3. _____ |
|---|---|---|---|
| What is your favorite holiday? Why? | | | |
| What is your favorite kind of weather? Why? | | | |
| What is your favorite season? Why? | | | |

# Answers

## Days and Dates (pg. 55)

1492   Columbus discovered the New World.

1620   The Pilgrims landed on Plymouth Rock and formed the Massachusetts Bay Colony.

1776   The Declaration of Independence was signed in the U.S.

## Crossword Puzzle (pg. 57)

**Across:**
1. watch
4. days
6. months
9. hours
10. weeks

**Down:**
2. hands
3. years
5. seconds
7. time
8. calendar

## Holidays (pg. 59)

1. party horns
2. Valentine cards
3. Easter eggs, Easter bunny
4. corsage
5. wreaths
6. flags
7. barbeques
8. ghosts, witches, jack-o'-lanterns
9. turkey
10. Christmas trees

# 5

# Shopping

# Fruits

*Practice this vocabulary with your teacher. Then fill in the blanks.*

_____

_____

_____

_____

_____

_____

_____

_____

_____

_____

_____

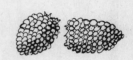

_____

| | | | |
|---|---|---|---|
| apple | grapefruit | orange | raspberries |
| banana | grapes | pear | strawberries |
| cherries | lemon | pineapple | watermelon |

## Questions for Conversation

*Practice asking and answering these questions with your teacher. Then ask your partner the questions.*

1. Which is your favorite fruit?

_____

2. Which fruits grow in your native country?

_____

3. Are there fruits which grow in your native country that don't grow in the United States? Which ones?

_____

4. Can you buy these fruits in your neighborhood?

_____

5. Which of these fruits do people sometimes slice and put in their tea?

_____

6. What other fruits do you like?

_____

# Vegetables

*Practice this vocabulary with your teacher. Then fill in the blanks.*

_____

_____

_____

_____

_____

_____

_____

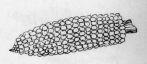

_____

_____

_____

_____

_____

| artichokes | broccoli | celery | onions |
| beans | cabbage | corn | peas |
| beets | carrots | lettuce | tomatoes |

## Questions for Conversation

*Practice asking and answering these questions with your teacher. Then ask your partner the questions.*

1. Which is your favorite vegetable?

   _____

2. Which vegetable do you like least?

   _____

3. Which vegetables do you usually use to prepare salad?

   _____

4. Which of these vegetables grow in your native country?

   _____

5. Where do you usually buy vegetables?

   _____

6. What other vegetables do you like?

   _____

# Meats, Poultry, Fish

*Practice this vocabulary with your teacher. Then fill in the blanks.*

_____

_____

_____

_____

_____

_____

_____

_____

_____

_____

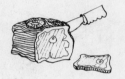

_____

_____

| chicken | hamburgers | roast beef | tripe |
| crab | pigs' feet | sausages | tuna fish |
| ham | pork chops | steak | turkey |

## Questions for Conversation

*Practice asking and answering these questions with your teacher. Then ask your partner the questions.*

1. What kind of meat do you eat most often?

   _____

2. Where do you usually buy meat?

   _____

3. What meat do you like to eat on special holidays like Christmas and Easter?

   _____

4. Do you eat fish?

   _____

5. What kind of fish is your favorite?

   _____

6. Where do you buy fish?

   _____

# Comparing Prices

## Comparison Shopping at the Supermarket

The small jar has half as much applesauce as the large one. Both jars are 99¢.
Which one is cheaper? Which one is the better buy?

Which can of peas is smaller?
Which can is cheaper?
Which can of peas is a better buy?

## Class Discussion

Some brands are famous. They are sold in many different stores. They are called **name brands.** Other brands are made especially for one supermarket chain. They are called **store brands.** Store brands are usually cheaper than name brands.

*Discuss with your class the name brands and store brands you know for each of these items. Are the name brands better than the store brands?*

1. bread
2. ketchup (catsup)
3. cheese
4. juices
5. Other: . . .

# Supermarket

## Vocabulary

*Practice this vocabulary with your teacher. Find all the words in the picture.*

| | | |
|---|---|---|
| aisle | cashier | clerk |
| groceries | deli counter | dairy section |
| shopping cart | paper bag | meat section |
| line | cash register | service window |

## With Your Partner

*Practice asking and answering these questions with your teacher. Then ask your partner the questions. Add one more question. Finally, report your interview to the class.*

1. Do you buy food in a supermarket? Which one?
2. Are the prices expensive or reasonable?
3. Do you ever buy anything at the deli (delicatessen) counter? What do you buy?
4. What dairy products do you buy?
5. What other sections are there in your supermarket?
6. Do you ever cash checks in the supermarket? Do you have a check-cashing card?
7. Are there supermarkets in your native country (or city)? Do they give paper bags to shoppers for groceries? What differences are there between a supermarket in your native country (or city) and a supermarket in the U.S.?
8. When is your supermarket the busiest? Why? When do you like to shop? Why?
9. What do you usually buy in the supermarket?
10. . . . . . . . . . . .

## Role Play: Paying the Cashier

Place: Supermarket check-out counter
Roles: Cashier, Shopper, "Bagger"
Props: Grocery bag, cans and boxes, table, big box (for cash register)

Action: Shopper puts food on table, Cashier checks it out. Bagger puts food into bag. Cashier asks for money. Shopper doesn't have enough. They decide what to do.

## Class Discussion: Saving Money at the Supermarket

*What are some ways you can save money at the supermarket? Talk about the pictures. Add your own idea.*

**75**

# Comparison Shopping

## Questions for Conversation

1. Where can you buy combs and brushes?

2. Where can you buy paper plates and cups? When do you use them?

3. Where can you buy paper towels? What can you use them for?

4. Where can you buy disposable diapers? How do you dispose of them when they are dirty?

5. Where can you buy deodorant? What brands do you know of?

6. What kinds of medicine can you buy in a supermarket?

7. What kind of tissues do you usually buy?

8. What kind of soap do you usually buy?

9. What kind of toothpaste do you usually buy?

10. What kind of shampoo do you usually buy?

## Community Activity

Is it cheaper to buy these items in one store than another? Compare the prices of the items on this page at two different stores in your community. Report to the class.

# Specialty Shops

_____    _____    _____    _____

_____    _____    _____

## Vocabulary

_Match the vocabulary with the items you can buy in **each** store._

| | | |
|---|---|---|
| card shop | magazine stand | lumberyard |
| fabric store | paint store | toy store |
| furniture store | | |

## Find Someone Who

_Ask the other students in your class if they have done these things. Find someone who has done each thing._

1. _____ has shopped in a lumberyard.
   _(What did he or she buy?)_

2. _____ has shopped in a card shop.
   _(What did he or she buy?)_

3. _____ has shopped in a furniture store.
   _(What did he or she buy?)_

4. _____ has shopped in a paint store.
   _(What did he or she buy?)_

5. _____ has shopped in a fabric store.
   _(What did he or she buy?)_

6. _____ has shopped in a toy store.
   _(What did he or she buy?)_

7. _____ has bought something at a magazine stand.
   _(What did he or she buy?)_

# Department Stores

**List on the Board: Shopping in a Department Store**

1. What can you buy in the **appliances department?**
2. What can you buy in the **housewares department?**
3. What can you buy in **men's wear?**
4. What can you buy in **misses?**
5. What can you buy in the **home entertainment department?**
6. What else can you buy in a department store?

**Questions for Conversation**

1. Do you ever shop in a department store? What is the name of the store?
2. Does the department store have elevators? Escalators? Which do you prefer?
3. Do you like to shop in department stores? Why or why not?
4. Do people shop in department stores in your native country? How are they different from department stores in the United States?

# What Size Do You Wear?

What is happening in these pictures?

Discuss these pictures with your class. Then fill in the blanks with the correct vocabulary.

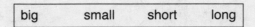

big    small    short    long

What size dress do *you* wear?

What size jacket do *you* wear?

What size hat do *you* wear?

What size pants do *you* wear?

# Questions for Conversation

1. Are sizes in the United States the same as sizes in your native country?
2. What size shirt do you take in the United States? In your native country?
3. What size coat do you take in the United States? In your native country?
4. What size shoes do you take in the United States? In your native country?
5. What is happening in this picture?

## Role Play: Shopping for Shoes

*Present this skit for your class with two other students.*

*Characters:* Customer, Friend, Salesclerk
*Place:* Shoestore
*Props:* Several chairs, several pairs of shoes

*Action:* The Customer and Friend come into the shoe store and look around. When they sit down, the Salesclerk asks to help them. The Customer tries on two pairs of shoes. The Customer and the Friend discuss the shoes. The Customer finally buys one pair.

# Sales and Advertisements

## Advertisements

*Read these two ads and discuss them with your class. Are they good sales?*

(Look for the regular price.)

(See if the sale is on first quality merchandise or **seconds** [damaged merchandise].)

## Pictures for Conversation: Sales

*What is happening in these pictures? Did you ever have a problem with a sale?*

## Community Exercise

*Bring fliers for sales to class. Read the fliers and find good sales.*

# Credit

*Fill in the blanks. Then read the paragraph with your class.*

| | | |
|---|---|---|
| charge | credit cards | finance charge |
| pay | bill | on time |

Many Americans have _____. They can _____ their purchases.

Usually, they do not have to _____ for the purchases until

the next month. Then they get a _____ in the mail for all

their purchases. If they don't pay _____ or if they don't pay

the whole bill, they have to pay a _____ (extra money)

the next month.

## Questions for Conversation

1. Do you have a credit card from a store? Which store?
2. Do you have a credit card from a bank? What is the name of the card?
3. Do you have a credit card from a gasoline company? Which one?
4. How do you apply for a credit card?
5. What percent (%) interest is the finance charge on your credit card?
6. Do people in your native country have credit cards? What kinds?

## Class Discussion

*Is it a good idea to use credit cards? List the advantages and disadvantages on the board.*

# Saving Money When You Go Shopping

## With Your Class

*Discuss these ways to save money.*

Shop in discount stores.

Shop during sales.

Buy new clothes to wear with your old ones.

Have special aprons and overalls for hard work.

Swap good things you don't need anymore.

Buy dark jackets and coats.

Follow label instructions.

Make your own clothes.

Buy washable clothes.

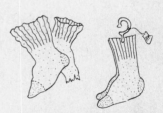

Buy socks and stockings in the same color.

How do you save money on clothes? Write an idea under this box and draw a picture.

# 6

# Your Community

# Services

Does your city or town have these services? Do you know where they are? Write the address, the telephone number, and the service.

Your city or town _____
(*or the closest city or town supplying the services*)

| Place | Address, City | Telephone | Service |
|---|---|---|---|
| Police Station | | | |
| Hospital *Name:* _____ | | | |
| Post Office | | | |
| Bank *Name:* _____ | | | |
| State Employment Office | | | |
| State Welfare Office | | | |
| State Registry of Motor Vehicles | | | |
| Public Library | | | |
| School *Name:* _____ | | | |
| Church *Name:* _____ | | | |
| Public Park *Name:* _____ | | | |
| Immigration Office | | | |
| Legal Aid Society | | | |
| Bus or Train Station | | | |

86

# Using the Telephone

## Instructions: Using a Pay Telephone for a Local Call*

*These instructions are not in the correct sequence. Read the instructions and number them in the correct order, 1 to 6.*

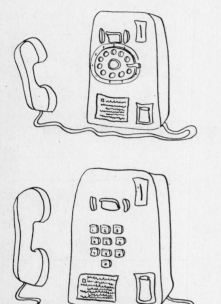

_____ Dial the number you want.

_____ Put a coin in the slot.

_____ When you finish your call, hang up the receiver.

_____ Take the receiver off the hook.

_____ If there is no answer, hang up and get your coin back from the change return.

_____ Wait for the dial tone.

*Practice saying these telephone numbers.*

1. 555-1212 <u>five five five one two one two</u>
2. 435-8300 <u>four three five eight three hundred (or three oh oh)**</u>
3. 326-8000 <u>three two six eight thousand (or eight oh oh oh)</u>
4. 927-8200 _____
5. 602-914-2000 _____
6. 716-659-8600 _____

*A local call is a call to the same city or a city close to the one you are calling from.

**Zero is usually called "oh" on the telephone, except when two or three zeros come together. See numbers 2 and 3 of this exercise.

# Calling for Assistance

What is the telephone number of the police station? Is there an emergency number?

_____

Did you ever call the police station?

When? _____

What do you say to the police officer on the telephone if your child is lost?

_____

_____

What is the telephone number of the fire station?

_____

What do you say to the firefighter on the telephone if your house is on fire?

_____

_____

What number do you dial if you need the operator?

_____

How can the operator help you?

_____

What is the telephone number of directory assistance?

_____

Why do you call directory assistance?

_____

_____

# Telephone Conversations

## With Your Partner

*Practice these telephone conversations with a partner and fill in the blanks together. Then present one of your conversations to the class.*

### Talking on The Telephone—Wrong Number

(Ring. . . . . .ring . . . . . .ring)

**A.** Hello.

**B.** Hello. May I speak to _____?

**A.** I'm sorry. You must have the wrong number.

**B.** Is this 374-0721?

**A.** No, it's not.

**B.** I'm sorry.

**A.** That's all right. Good-bye.

**B.** Good-bye.

### Taking a Message

(Ring. . . . . .ring . . . . . .ring)

**A.** Hello.

**B.** Hello. This is _____. Is Jim there?

**A.** No, he's not here right now. May I take a message?

**B.** Yes. Please ask him to call me at 891-5432.

**A.** Was that 891-5432?

**B.** Yes.

**A.** Please spell your name for me.

**B.** _ _ _ _ _ _ _

**A.** Fine. I'll give Jim the message. Good-bye.

**B.** Thank you. Good-bye.

### Talking to Your Friend

(Ring. . . . . .ring. . . . . .ring)

**A.** Hello.

**B.** Hello, _____ How are you?
     *(your friend's name)*

**A.** Fine, thanks. . . . . . . . . . . . . . . . . . . . . . . . . . . . . . . . . . . . .

**B.** No, I can't go to the movies tonight. I have a class.

**A.** Why don't you call _____?
     *(another student's name)*

**B.** . . . . . . . . . . . . . . . . . . . . . . . . . . . . . . . . . . . . . . . . . . .

**A.** Bye. See you tomorrow.

# Using the Telephone Directory

*Find the addresses and telephone numbers of the places below in the telephone book:*

|  | Address | Telephone number |
|---|---|---|
| A television technician |  |  |
| A tire store |  |  |
| A local church |  |  |
| The telephone company business office |  |  |
| A paint store |  |  |
| A plumber |  |  |
| Your favorite restaurant |  |  |
| A travel agency |  |  |
| A movie theater |  |  |
| A drug store |  |  |
| (Other) |  |  |

## Circle Dialogue

**Do a circle dialogue with the question, "When do you call a . . . . .?"**

Teacher: "When do you call a plumber?"

Student 1: "I call a plumber when my sink is broken. When do you call a **tire store?**"

Student 2: I call a **tire store** when I need information about tires. When do you call . . . . .?"

*Continue around the circle.*

# Talking to Your Landlord

*Discuss this situation with your class. Then fill in the blanks and choose two students to role play this conversation for the class.*

(Dial your landlord's number.)

Landlord: Hello.

Tenant: Hello. This is _____. May I speak with _____, please?

Landlord: Speaking. What can I do for you?

Tenant: ...............................................................

...............................................................

...............................................................

Landlord: ...............................................................

...............................................................

...............................................................

Tenant: ...............................................................

...............................................................

...............................................................

Landlord: ...............................................................

# What Do You Say:
# At the Post Office
# At School Registration

## Role Play

*Discuss these situations with your class. Then complete the dialogues with a partner. Role play your dialogue for the class.*

## At the Post Office

Postal worker: Good morning. May I help you?

Customer: . . . . . . . . . . . . . . . . . . . . . . . . . . . . . . . . . . . . . . . . . . . . . .

Postal worker: Here they are. That's $1.96, please.

Customer: . . . . . . . . . . . . . . . . . . . . . . . . . . . . . . . . . . . . . . . . . . . . . .

Postal worker: Here's your change. Have a good day!

Customer: . . . . . . . . . . . . . . . . . . . . . . . . . . . . . . . . . . . . . . . . . . . . . .

## At School Registration

**Situation**: You are at elementary school to register your child for kindergarten.

Parent: Hello. My name is . . . . . . . . . . I want to register my child for kindergarten.

Secretary: Hello. Please have a seat. Do you have his immunization record and birth certificate?

Parent: . . . . . . . . . . . . . . . . . . . . . . . . . . . . . . . . . . . . . . . . . . . . . . . . .

Secretary: Fine. I'll need to see proof of residence, too. Do you have a copy of your lease?

Parent: . . . . . . . . . . . . . . . . . . . . . . . . . . . . . . . . . . . . . . . . . . . . . . . . .

Secretary: Good. Just fill out this registration form.

Parent: . . . . . . . . . . . . . . . . . . . . . . . . . . . . . . . . . . . . . . . . . . . . . . . . .

Secretary: No, that's all. We'll see you and your child on September 6th at 8:00. Have a nice summer.

Parent: . . . . . . . . . . . . . . . . . . . . . . . . . . . . . . . . . . . . . . . . . . . . . . . . .

# What Do You Say:
# At the Supermarket
# At the Hospital

This man works in a supermarket. He's a stockboy. If you want to buy three pounds of onions, what do you say to him?

.................................................

.................................................

This woman works in a hospital. She's a receptionist. You have a sick friend in the hospital. You come to visit. If you do not know what room your friend is in, what do you say to her?

.................................................

.................................................

## Role Plays

*What is happening in these pictures? Discuss them with your class. Then fill in the blanks with a partner and role play the conversation for the class.*

## Questions for Conversation

1. Do you ever say anything in the supermarket? What do you say?
2. Were you ever in a hospital? What for? Did you have to ask any questions? What questions?
3. Do you ever go to the post office? What do you do there? What do you say?
4. Did you ever register yourself or your child for school? Tell the class about it.

**93**

# What Do You Say:
# At a Gas Station
# At the Library

## Role Plays

*What is happening in these pictures? Discuss them with your class. Then fill in the blanks with a partner and role-play one conversation for the class.*

This woman works in a gas station. She's a gas station attendant. If the gas tank in your car is empty and you think the car needs oil, what do you say to her?

...........................................

...........................................

These women work in the library. They're librarians. If you are looking for a local newspaper in your native language, what do you say to them?

...........................................

...........................................

## Questions for Conversation

1.  Do you ever go to a library? What do you do there?
2.  Do you ever stop at a gas station? What do you do there? What do you say?

# Solving Problems:
# At a Bank
# In a Restaurant

## Role Play

*Discuss these problems with your class. Then fill in the blanks with a partner and role-play one problem for the class.*

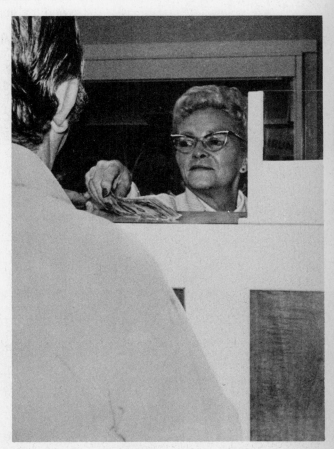

This woman works in a restaurant. She's a waitress. You order a sandwich and coffee. If she brings you the sandwich but does not bring the coffee, what do you say to her?

.................................................

.................................................

This woman works in a bank. She's a teller. If you are cashing a check for $50.00 and she gives you $40.00, what do you say to her?

.................................................

.................................................

## Class Discussion: Problems

Did you ever have a problem with communication in a restaurant? In a bank? At the post office? At school? At a super-market? In a hospital? At a gas station? In a library?
What was the problem? How did you solve it?

# Giving Directions

*With your group, look at the map on the facing page. Practice giving directions to the different places in this neighborhood. (Numbers 1., 2., and 3. are done for you.)*

If you are at your house on the corner of **Maple Street** and **First Avenue** (see (**a**) on the map), how do you get to:

1. *Central Park:* Walk straight down Maple Street, past the Protestant Church and the library on the left.

2. *School:* Walk down First Avenue for one block. The school is on the left.

3. *Shopping Mall:* Walk down Maple Street. Take the shortcut through the park. Walk one block on Elm Street.

4. *Catholic Church:* _____

_____


If you are at the bus station (see **b**), how do you get to:

5. *School:* _____

_____

6. *Library:* _____

_____

7. *Police Station:* _____

_____


If you are at the shopping mall (see **c**), how do you get to:

8. *Greek Church:* _____

_____

9. *School:* _____

_____

10. *Your house:* _____

_____

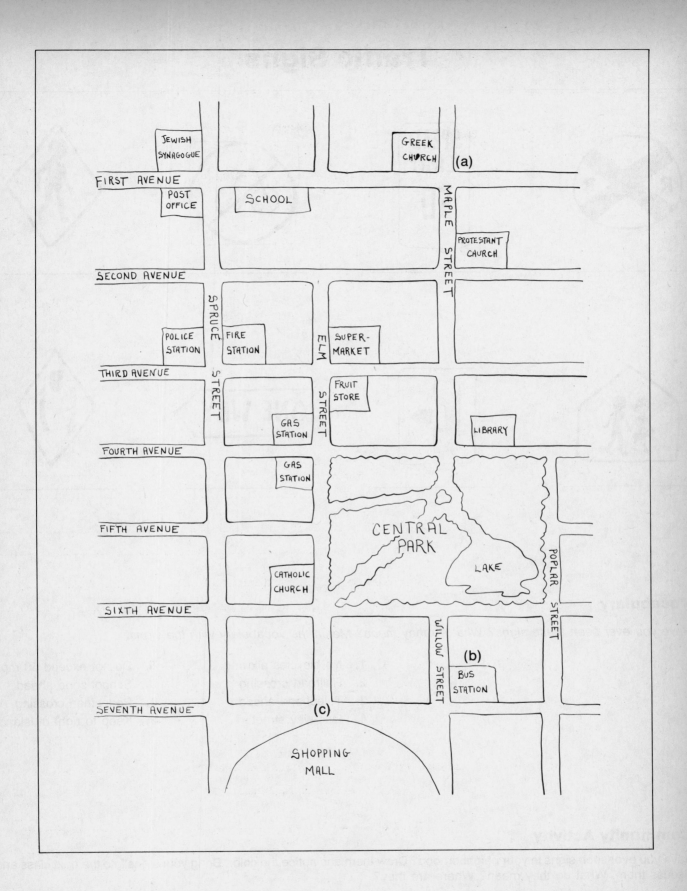

**97**

# Traffic Signs

  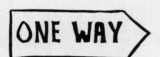 

## Vocabulary

*Have you ever seen these signs? What do they mean? Match the vocabulary with the signs.*

1. No bicycles allowed
2. Railroad crossing
3. Telephone ahead
4. One-way street

5. Do not exceed 50 mph
6. School zone ahead
7. Pedestrian crossing
8. Keep to right of island

## Community Activity

Have you ever seen signs in your neighborhood? Draw them and notice the color. Bring your signs into the next class and discuss them. What do they mean? Where are they?

# Your Car

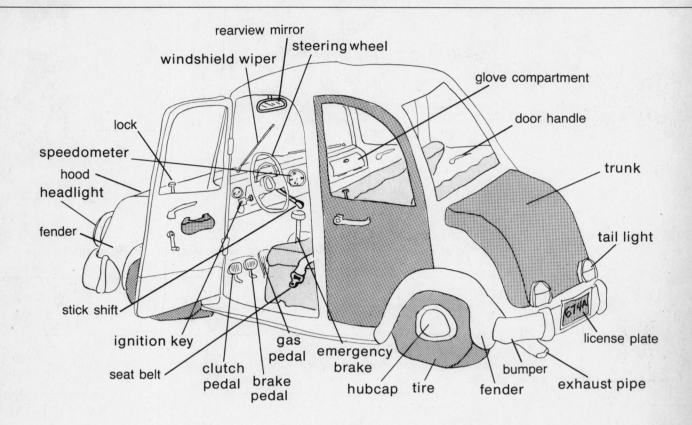

## Vocabulary

Practice this vocabulary with your teacher.

## With Your Partner

*Practice asking and answering these questions with your teacher. Then ask your partner the questions.*

1. Do you know how to drive a car?
2. Do you have a license?
3. Can you drive a standard shift?
4. Do you have a car? What kind?
5. What kinds of cars do people drive in your native country?
6. What kind of car would you like to drive?

What does the man in this cartoon do with his car when he wants to park it?

_____

Why is the police officer waiting?

_____

What do you think the police officer is thinking?

_____

Would you like to be able to do this too? Why?

_____

## Class Discussion

Is parking a problem where you live? How do you solve it?

# Public Transportation

*Read this with your class.*

Many cities in the United States have public transportation.

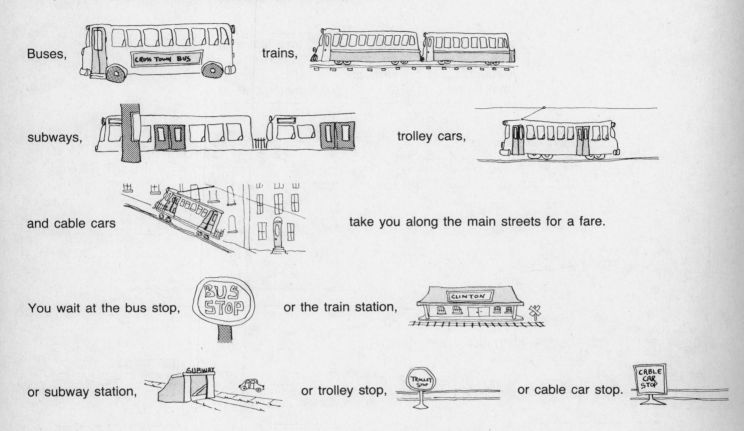

Buses, trains,

subways, trolley cars,

and cable cars take you along the main streets for a fare.

You wait at the bus stop, or the train station,

or subway station, or trolley stop, or cable car stop.

In some cities, you have to pay the fare at the beginning of the trip and in some cities you pay at the end. Public transportation is convenient because you don't have to own a car or use taxis, which can be expensive.

## Questions for Conversation

1. What kind of public transportation is there in your community?
2. Do you ever use it? When?
3. How much is the **fare**? Can you use a **token**?
4. What public transportation is there in your native country?
5. Do many people use it?
6. How is it different from public transportation in the United States?
7. Which kind of public transportation do you prefer?

## Community Activity

*Bring in bus and train schedules for reading and discussion.*

# Long Distance Travel

## Vocabulary

*Practice this vocabulary with your teacher and fill in the blank under each picture.*

| | | |
|---|---|---|
| car | ship | train station |
| train | on foot | airport |
| rowboat | sailboat | dock |
| small plane | jet | motorboat |

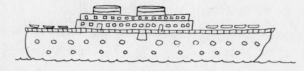
_____

_____

_____

_____

_____

_____

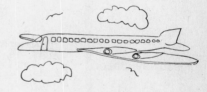
_____

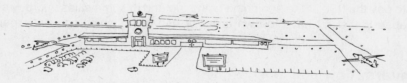
_____

_____

_____

_____

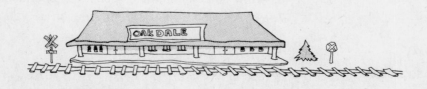
_____

## Find Someone Who

*Find someone in your class who has done these things.*

1. Who has taken a long trip by plane? Where? When? _____
   _____

2. Who has taken a long voyage on a ship? Where? How long? _____
   _____

3. Who has taken a long voyage in a small boat? When? How long? Tell about
   it. _____
   _____

4. Who has been to the airport recently? Why was he or she there? _____
   _____

5. Who has taken a long train trip? Where? How long did it take? _____
   _____

6. Who has traveled a long way on foot? Where? How far? _____
   _____

# 7

# Jobs

# What Is Your Job?

What are the people doing in these pictures? Would you like to have any of these jobs?

He's a **painter.**

He's a **police officer.**

She's a **doctor.**

He's a **T.V. technician.**

She's a **housewife.**

## With Your Partner

*Ask your partner these questions.*

1. What is your job?
2. Where do you work?
3. What hours do you work?
4. Do you like your job?
5. Do you have a **social security card?**
6. What is your **social security number?**
7. Do you have a **green card?**

# Occupations

## Vocabulary

*These people are working. What are their occupations?\* Repeat the vocabulary with your teacher. Fill in the blanks, then read the sentences together.*

| | | | |
|---|---|---|---|
| babysitter | teacher | truckdriver | waiter |
| singer | baseball player | dancer | factory worker |
| farmer | baker | bartender | photographer |

1. She teaches in school. She's a _____.

2. He works in a factory. He's a _____.

3. He drives a tractor on a farm. He's a _____.

4. She takes care of children. She's a _____.

5. He tends bar in a restaurant. He's a _____.

6. He photographs people in a studio. He's a _____.

\*Occupation = Job

7. She sings song in a nightclub. She's a _____.

8. He bakes bread in a bakery. He's a _____.

9. He plays baseball on a baseball team. He's a _____.

10. He waits on tables in a restaurant. He's a _____.

11. He drives a truck. He's a _____.

12. She dances on stages. She's a _____.

## Pantomime Game

*Student 1 begins by acting out one of the jobs below. When another student guesses the correct job, he or she must also tell what the worker does. All students write what he or she says on the corresponding line. Example: (Student 1 acts out a teacher. Student 2 guesses correctly.) Student 2 says "A teacher teaches." All students write, "A teacher teaches." Then Student 2 acts out another job. Continue until all jobs are filled in.*

1. teacher _A teacher teaches._____
2. mail carrier _____
3. salesperson _____
4. bus driver _____
5. student _____
6. factory worker _____
7. baker _____
8. waiter _____
9. football player _____
10. your job _____

(name of your job)

**107**

# Where Do They Work?

*Answer these questions with your class.*

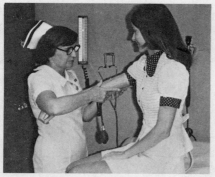

Where does a **nurse** work?

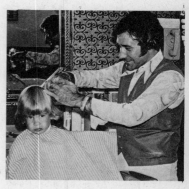

Where does a **barber** work?

Where does a **shoe salesperson** work?

Where does a **butcher** work?

## Circle Dialogue

*Do this circle dialogue with your group. Continue with all the occupations in this chapter.*

Student 1: Where does a barber work?
Student 2: In a barber shop. Where does a butcher work?
Student 3: In a butcher shop. Where does a _____ work?

**108**

# Finding a Job

## Vocabulary

*Fill in the blanks. Then read with your teacher.*

| classified section | employment counselor |
| computer job bank | newspaper |
| help wanted sign | |

*This woman is looking at a _____ _____ _____ in a window. She will go inside the restaurant and apply for the job as a waitress.*

*This man is reading a help wanted ad in a _____. The ads for jobs are in the _____.*

*This man is studying a _____ _____ _____ with an _____ _____. He is at a state employment office.*

## With Your Partner

*Practice asking and answering these questions with your teacher. Then ask your partner the questions. Add another question with your partner. Finally, report your interview to the class.*

1. Have you ever found a job through:
   the state employment office job bank?
   a classified advertisement in a newspaper?
   a sign in a window?
   an employment agency?
   a friend?
   other? _____

2. How did you find the job you have now?
3. What do you think is the best way to find a job?
4. ...................................................

## Community Activity

*Read the* Help Wanted *section of a local newspaper together and answer these questions:*

1. What kinds of jobs are available?
2. How much do they pay?
3. Do they require English?
   Do they require your native language?
4. Do they require a **high school diploma?**
5. Do they require **special training?**
6. Do they provide **on-the-job** training?
7. Are there any **unskilled labor** jobs?
   What are the jobs?
8. Are there any good job openings for you?
   What are they?
9. What type of job do you want to find?

# Employment Application

**PERSONAL**

| LAST NAME | FIRST | INITIAL | TODAY'S DATE | SOCIAL SECURITY NUMBER |
|---|---|---|---|---|

PRESENT ADDRESS (STREET, CITY, STATE, ZIP CODE) | AREA CODE/HOME TELEPHONE

ARE YOU OVER THE MINIMUM LEGAL AGE? | ARE YOU IN THE U.S. ON A VISA WHICH PROHIBITS YOU FROM WORKING HERE? ☐ YES ☐ NO  TYPE VISA | HAVE YOU PREVIOUSLY APPLIED? ☐ NO ☐ YES  WHEN?

HAVE YOU BEEN CONVICTED OF ANY LAW VIOLATION WHICH BEARS A RELATIONSHIP TO THE JOB FOR WHICH YOU ARE APPLYING AND WHICH HAS NOT BEEN ANNULLED OR SEALED BY A COURT? ☐ NO ☐ YES | IF YES, PLEASE EXPLAIN:

**EMPLOYMENT**

BUSINESS TELEPHONE NUMBER AND EXTENSION WHERE YOU CAN BE REACHED | POSITION APPLIED FOR ☐ FULL-TIME ☐ PART-TIME | SALARY DESIRED $ | DATE YOU COULD START

| FROM mo. yr. | TO mo. yr. | PREVIOUS EMPLOYERS (Most Recent First) NAME  ADDRESS | NAME OF SUPERVISOR AND TITLE | YOUR POSITION | SALARY Beginning | Last | REASON FOR LEAVING |
|---|---|---|---|---|---|---|---|
| | | | | | | | |
| | | | | | | | |
| | | | | | | | |
| | | | | | | | |

MAY WE CONTACT YOUR PRESENT EMPLOYER? ☐ YES ☐ NO

**EDUCATION**

| FROM mo. yr. | TO mo. yr. | NAME AND ADDRESS OF SCHOOL | TYPE COURSE OR MAJOR / MINOR | HIGHEST GRADE COMPLETED | DEGREE | YEAR AWARDED |
|---|---|---|---|---|---|---|
| | | HIGH OR PREP 1. | | | | |
| | | 2. | | | | |
| | | BUSINESS OR SPECIAL | | | | |
| | | COLLEGE 1. | | | | |
| | | 2. | | | | |
| | | GRADUATE SCHOOL 1. | | | | |
| | | 2. | | | | |
| | | LAW SCHOOL | ARE YOU A MEMBER OF THE BAR? ☐ YES ☐ NO  IF "YES", WHAT STATES? ____  WHEN ADMITTED? | | | |

**SKILLS**

TYPING SPEED _____ WORDS PER MINUTE          STENO SPEED _____ WORDS PER MINUTE

BUSINESS MACHINES YOU CAN OPERATE _____

LIST ANY SPECIAL SKILLS YOU MAY HAVE _____

*PLEASE COMPLETE REVERSE SIDE*

**HONORS**

| HONORS, AWARDS, PUBLICATIONS AND TECHNICAL SOCIETIES | | | TRAINING AND DEVELOPMENT PROGRAMS | | |
|---|---|---|---|---|---|
| TYPE OR NAME | WHERE | DATE | TYPE | TAKEN AT | DATE |
| | | | | | |
| | | | | | |
| | | | | | |

**REFERRALS**

| REFERRED BY (INDICATE NAME) | EMPLOYEE | EMPLOYMENT AGENCY |
|---|---|---|
| | COLLEGE | CIVIC OR GOVERNMENT AGENCY |
| | NEWSPAPER AD | ON MY OWN |

**GOALS**

BRIEFLY DESCRIBE CAREER OBJECTIVES

_____

_____

_____

_____

**SIGNATURE**

THANK YOU VERY MUCH FOR COMPLETING OUR APPLICATION. PLEASE TAKE A FEW MINUTES TO READ THE FOLLOWING STATEMENT AND ADD YOUR SIGNATURE IN THE SPACE PROVIDED.

I UNDERSTAND THAT IF I AM EMPLOYED AND IF ANY STATEMENT HEREIN IS NOT TRUE, I MAY BE RELEASED IMMEDIATELY. IN ADDITION, I UNDERSTAND THAT THE FIRST THREE MONTHS OF MY EMPLOYMENT ARE A PROBATIONARY PERIOD AND THAT I MAY BE RELEASED DURING THIS PERIOD WITHOUT NOTICE OR SEVERANCE PAY.

APPLICANT'S SIGNATURE _____ DATE _____

**COMPANY USE ONLY**

PERSONNEL INTERVIEWER

DEPARTMENT INTERVIEWER

*TO BE COMPLETED BY HIRING DEPARTMENT HEAD*

| START DATE | DIV. / DEPT. CODE | DIV. / DEPT. NAME | LOCATION (BUILDING & FLOOR) |
|---|---|---|---|
| | | | |

| JOB TITLE (USE GENERIC TITLE ONLY) | EXT. EMPLOYEE CAN BE REACHED ON | SUPERVISOR'S NAME |
|---|---|---|
| | | |

| B/W STARTING SALARY | BASED ON 35 37½ 40 ☐ ☐ ☐ HOUR WK. | HOURLY STARTING RATE | INCENTIVE NO ☐ YES ☐ | EXEMPT ( IF YES, ATTACH EXEMPTION FORM ) NO ☐ YES ☐ ADMIN. ☐ EXEC. ☐ PROF. ☐ |
|---|---|---|---|---|
| $ | | $ PER HR. | | |

D.H. SIGNATURE / DATE

4.1/1648 (5/82)

# Benefits

## Vocabulary

*Fill in the blanks. Then read with your teacher.*

| | |
|---|---|
| vacation | unemployment insurance |
| paid holidays | worker's compensation |
| health insurance | pension |
| retirement | maternity leave |

This man is sick. His hospital and doctor bills are paid by _____ _____ benefits.

This elderly man is retired. He receives a _____ benefit check every month.

These people are out of work. They are waiting in line to receive _____ _____ benefit checks.

This family has a day off from work for Independence Day. They are enjoying a _____ _____ benefit.

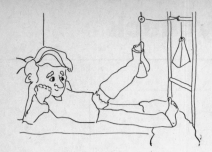

This man was injured at work. His sick leave and medical bills are covered by _____ _____ benefits.

This woman is pregnant. She can stay away from work to have her baby and return to work later because she has a _____ _____ benefit.

This man is relaxing on the beach for a week but he will still receive his regular paycheck from work. He is enjoying a _____ benefit.

## With Your Partner

*Practice asking and answering these questions with your teacher. Then ask your partner the questions. Add another question with your partner. Finally, report your interview to the class.*

1. Do you receive fringe benefits on your job? Which benefits?
2. If you don't receive benefits, how can you get health insurance?
3. What benefits do employees usually receive in your native country?

4. Do full-time employees receive benefits in your native country? Do part-time employees receive benefits?
5. Which benefits do you think are most important?
6. ................................................

## Class Discussion

*Did you ever use any fringe benefits from your job? Tell the class about your experience.*

## Class Discussion

*Fill in the blanks. Then read and discuss.*

| | |
|---|---|
| union | working conditions |
| strike | wages |
| contract | |

These people are members of a _____. The union makes a _____ with the employer. It helps to improve _____ _____ and _____. If the union and the employer cannot agree, the union goes on _____.

113

# Deductions from Your Paycheck

1. What is the difference between **gross earnings** and **net earnings**?
2. Your employer pays for some **fringe benefits.** You pay for other **fringe benefits** through **deductions** from your paycheck. Some fringe benefits both you and your employer pay for together.

Which benefits do you pay for?* _____

Which benefits does your employer pay for?* _____

Which benefits do you both pay for?* _____

Look at this pay stub. Do you understand each of the deductions? Does your pay stub look like this?

| HOURS WORKED | OVERTIME PREMIUM HOURS | PAID ABSENCE HOURS | HOLIDAY VACATION HOURS | SHORT WEEK HOURS | MISC. HOURS | BASE PAY | OVERTIME PREMIUM PAY | NIGHT PREMIUM PAY | PRIOR WEEKS ADJUSTMENT |
|---|---|---|---|---|---|---|---|---|---|
| 52 7 | 6 35 | | | | | 178 64 | 19 32 | 10 56 | |

| | SHORT WEEK PAY | GROSS EARNINGS | FEDERAL WITHHOLD. TAX | STATE TAX | F.I.C.A. | OTHER TAX | UNION DUES | CONTRIBUTION |
|---|---|---|---|---|---|---|---|---|
| THIS WEEK | | 208 52 | 41 80 | 10 39 | 12 97 | | 9 18 | 1 25 |
| THIS YEAR | | 1894 36 | 334 67 | 88 42 | 131 82 | | 45 78 | |

| GARNISHMENTS | CREDIT UNION | TOOLS GLASSES SHOES | U.S. SAVINGS BONDS | SPECIAL DEPEND. INSUR. | PAID ABSENCE BALANCE | LOCK BADGE | NET PAY | SPECIAL DEDUCTIONS | PAY PERIOD END |
|---|---|---|---|---|---|---|---|---|---|
| | 10 00 | | | | | | 122 93 | | MO. 04 DAY 30 YR. 85 |

| EMPLOYEE NUMBER | DEPT. | SECTION | |
|---|---|---|---|
| 01793 | 42 | 5 | MIDDLETON ELECTRONICS CORPORATION |

KEEP THIS CARD — it is your STATEMENT OF EARNINGS

If your employer provides **room** and **board,** he or she will also deduct these from your paycheck.

*See page 118 for the answers.

# Paying Taxes

In the United States, every January your employer mails you a W-2 form (Wage and Tax Statement). You must send this form with your income tax forms to the Internal Revenue Service by April 15th.

| For Official Use Only | | Wage and Tax Statement<br>See instructions on Form W-3 and back of Copy D | | **1984** |
|---|---|---|---|---|
| ACME MACHINE SHOP<br>90 STATE STREET<br>ANYTOWN, U.S.A. 99999 | | Type or print EMPLOYER'S name, address, ZIP code and Federal (State) identifying number. | **Copy A For Internal Revenue Service Center**<br>* See instructions on back of Copy D. | |
| Employee's social security number<br>016-23-7384 | 1 Federal income tax withheld<br>$ 1345.91 | 2 Wages, tips, and other compensation<br>$ 9462 | 3 FICA employee tax withheld<br>$ 553.53 | 4 Total FICA wages |
| **21** ☐ | | | | |
| Type or print EMPLOYEE'S name, address, and ZIP code below (Name must aline with arrow) | | 5 Was employee covered by a qualified pension plan, etc.? | 6 * | 7 * |
| **Name ▶** Joseph Melia<br>14 Main Street<br>Anytown, U.S.A 99999 | | 8 State tax withheld<br>$ 47.31 | 9 State wages | 10 State |
| Form **W-2** | | 11 City or local | 12 City or local | 13 City or locality |

APPROVED I.R.S.    Department of the Treasury—Internal Revenue Service   13-2581759

## Questions

*What is this form? Discuss these questions with your class.*

1. What is Joseph Melia's social security number?
2. How much money did Joseph Melia earn in 1984?
   What was his gross income? (#2)
   What was his net income? (#2 minus #1=net income)
3. How much was withheld from his wages?
   federal (#1)
   state (#8)

# Losing Your Job

## Pictures for Discussion

There are many reasons for losing a job. You may be **laid off** because business is slow, or because the company is closing down. You may be **fired** for excessive absence, fighting, stealing, or other unacceptable behavior. If you are a temporary employee, you may be **terminated** automatically at the end of a certain period.

*What is happening in each of the pictures below?*

# Crossword Puzzle

*Fill in this crossword puzzle.*

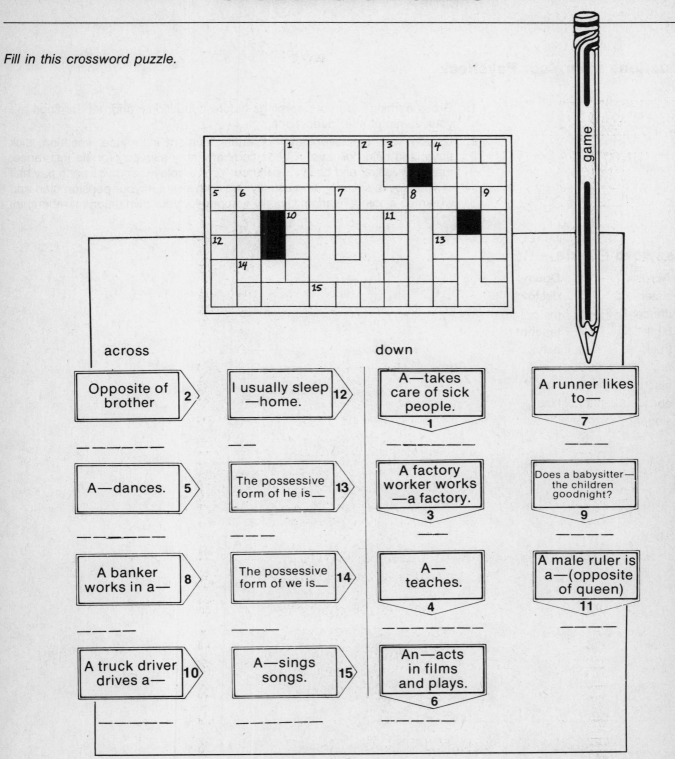

across

| | |
|---|---|
| Opposite of brother | 2 |

_ _ _ _ _ _

| | |
|---|---|
| A—dances. | 5 |

_ _ _ _ _ _

| | |
|---|---|
| A banker works in a— | 8 |

_ _ _ _ _ _

| | |
|---|---|
| A truck driver drives a— | 10 |

_ _ _ _ _ _

| | |
|---|---|
| I usually sleep —home. | 12 |

_ _ _ _

| | |
|---|---|
| The possessive form of he is— | 13 |

_ _ _ _

| | |
|---|---|
| The possessive form of we is— | 14 |

_ _ _ _

| | |
|---|---|
| A—sings songs. | 15 |

_ _ _ _ _ _

down

| | |
|---|---|
| A—takes care of sick people. | 1 |

_ _ _ _ _

| | |
|---|---|
| A factory worker works —a factory. | 3 |

_ _

| | |
|---|---|
| A— teaches. | 4 |

_ _ _ _ _ _ _

| | |
|---|---|
| An—acts in films and plays. | 6 |

_ _ _ _ _

| | |
|---|---|
| A runner likes to— | 7 |

_ _ _

| | |
|---|---|
| Does a babysitter— the children goodnight? | 9 |

_ _ _ _

| | |
|---|---|
| A male ruler is a—(opposite of queen) | 11 |

See pg. 118 for the answers.

**117**

# Answers

## Deductions from Your Paycheck

1. Gross earnings are your earnings before deductions, and net earnings are your earnings after deductions.

2. Usually your employer pays for unemployment insurance, vacation, sick days, and paid holidays. A large company may also pay for life insurance, maternity leave, and health insurance. Your employer and you each pay half of your social security, and usually you both share in your pension plan and workmen's compensation. Usually you pay for your own union membership.

## Crossword Puzzle

| Across | | Down | |
|---|---|---|---|
| 2. | sister | 1. | doctor |
| 5. | dancer | 3. | in |
| 8. | bank | 4. | teacher |
| 10. | truck | 6. | actor |
| 12. | at | 7. | run |
| 13. | his | 9. | kiss |
| 14. | our | 11. | king |
| 15. | singer | | |

# 8

# Health

# Inside Your Body

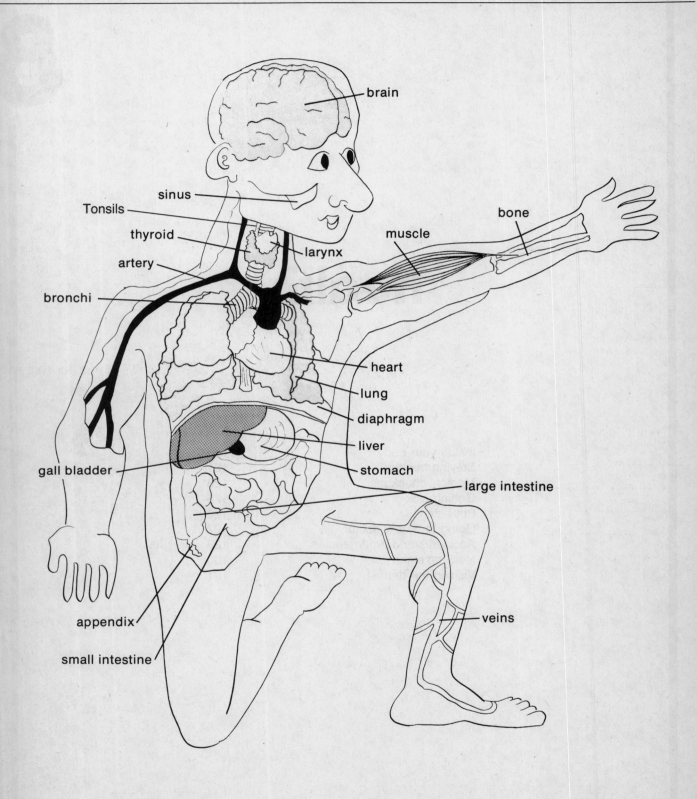

- brain
- sinus
- Tonsils
- thyroid
- larynx
- artery
- bronchi
- muscle
- bone
- heart
- lung
- diaphragm
- liver
- stomach
- gall bladder
- large intestine
- appendix
- small intestine
- veins

# Staying Healthy

## With Your Group

*Talk with your class about these ways to stay healthy. Then in groups of four or five, fill in the charts. Finally, write a master list on the board.*

1. ***Eat nutritious foods and regular meals.*** How many nutritious meals do you eat every day? Ask your partners and fill in the chart.

| Student's Name | Number of nutritious meals |
| --- | --- |
|  |  |
|  |  |
|  |  |
|  |  |

2. ***Get plenty of exercise.*** What do you do for exercise? Ask your partners and fill in the chart.

| Student's Name | Exercise |
| --- | --- |
|  |  |
|  |  |
|  |  |
|  |  |

3. ***Get enough sleep.*** How many hours a night do you usually sleep? Ask your partners and fill in the chart.

| Student's Name | Hours of sleep |
| --- | --- |
|  |  |
|  |  |
|  |  |
|  |  |

**4.** *Have regular checkups.* Did you ever have a checkup? When? Where? Ask your partners and fill in the chart.

| Student's Name | Date of last checkup |
|---|---|
| | |
| | |
| | |
| | |

**5a.** *Dress properly.* What do you wear when it's cold? Ask your partners and fill in the chart.

| Student's Name | Clothing (for cold weather) |
|---|---|
| | |
| | |
| | |
| | |

**5b.** What do you wear when it's hot? Ask your partners and fill in the chart.

| Student's Name | Clothing (for hot weather) |
|---|---|
| | |
| | |
| | |
| | |

**6.** *Use drugs wisely.* What drugs do you use? Ask your partners and fill in the chart.

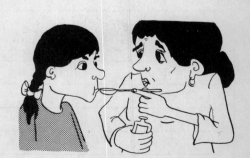

| Student's Name | Drugs |
|---|---|
| | |
| | |
| | |
| | |

# Medical Checkups

These children are not sick. They are having their checkups with the doctor. The doctor and nurse are examining them to be sure they are healthy and growing properly.

**What Is the Doctor Doing?**

*Match the correct sentence with the corresponding photograph.*

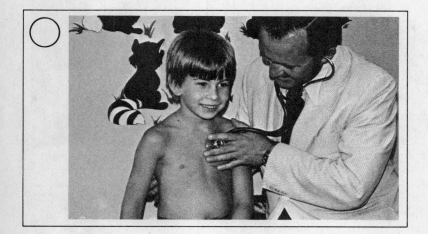

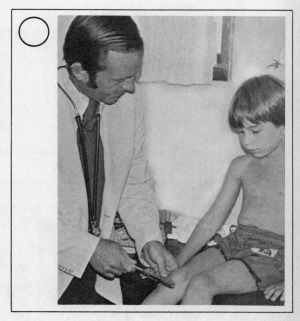

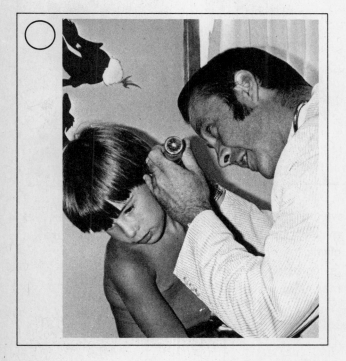

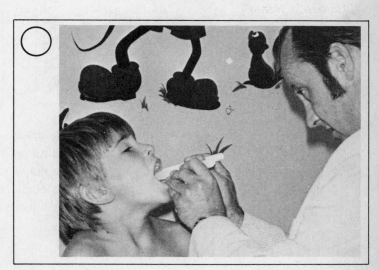

1. The doctor is examining the boy's throat with a **flashlight** and a **tongue depressor.**
2. The doctor is listening to the boy's heart with a **stethoscope.**
3. The doctor is checking the boy's **reflexes.**
4. The doctor is checking the boy's ears.

**What Is the Nurse Doing?**

*Match the correct sentence with the corresponding photograph.*

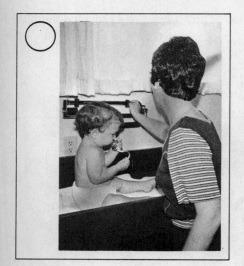
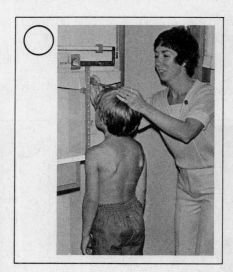
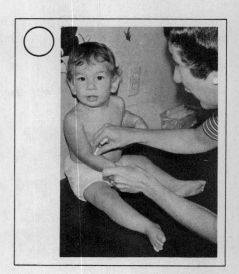

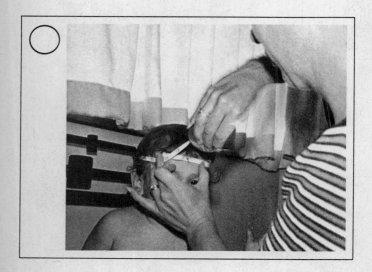
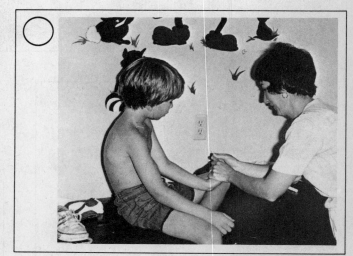

1. The nurse is weighing the baby on a special scale for babies.
2. The nurse is measuring the baby's head with a **tape measure**.
3. The nurse is giving the baby a **tine test**.
4. The nurse is taking blood for a **blood test**.
5. The nurse is measuring the boy.

## Questions for Conversation

1. When do you get a checkup?
2. What does the nurse do?
3. What does the doctor do?
4. Do adults have checkups in your native country? Where?
5. Do children have checkups in your native country? When? Where?
6. What does the doctor do? What does the nurse do?

**124**

# Getting Sick

*Fill in the blanks. Then read with your teacher.*

| laryngitis | toothache | cold |
|---|---|---|
| sore throat | backache | headache |
| fever | earache | stomachache |

My head aches.

He has a _____

My tooth hurts.

She has a _____

My ear hurts.

He has an _____

I can't talk.

She has _____

My nose is stuffy.

He has a _____

My throat hurts.

She has a _____

My stomach hurts.

He has a _____

My back hurts.

She has a _____

I'm hot and achy.

He has a _____

## Pantomime

*Students sit in a circle and take turns pantomiming the different symptoms while the rest of the group guesses what's wrong.*

## Circle Dialogue

*Students take turns asking and answering these questions about common symptoms and ailments.*

Teacher:   "My head aches. What's the matter with me?"
Student 1:   "You have a headache. My tooth hurts. What's the matter with me?"

*Continue around the circle.*

## List on the Board: What Do You Do When You Are Sick?

*Discuss with the class what you do when you have any of these ailments. Write the remedies on the board.*

# Physicians

## Role Play

*Below is a list of doctors from the telephone directory. Find the appropriate doctor for each situation. Choose one doctor. Role-play calling the doctor's office. Make an appointment or explain to the doctor what's wrong and ask for advice.*

1. You have a skin rash. _____

2. You get headaches when you watch T.V. or drive. _____

3. You need an X-ray to complete the medical requirements of a new job. _____

4. You are sad and lonely all the time. _____

5. You are going to have a baby. _____

6. You think your child has hay fever. _____

7. Your back hurts. _____

8. You had a heart attack and need a checkup. _____

9. You need an operation. _____

10. You are new in town and need a new doctor. _____

**Anderson, Arthur**
Surgery
Office hours by appointment
Parkview Building . . . . . . . . 345-3456

**Alexander, Gregory**
Psychiatry
Office hours by appointment
39 Burril St. . . . . . . . . . . . . . 235-5407

**Banner, Randall**
Hematology
10 Berry St. . . . . . . . . . . . . . 389-2243

**Carpenter, David**
Pediatrics
Office hours by appointment
34 Andover St. . . . . . . . . . . 345-2287

**Clopper, Benjamin**
Orthopedist
256 Lafayette St.
By appointment only . . . . . . 389-7714

**Cummings, Marcia**
Dermatologist and skin disorders
By appointment only
23 Nahant St. . . . . . . . . . . . . 346-6733

**Cunningham, Peter**
General practitioner
457 Main St. . . . . . . . . . . . . . 345-5003

**Dalby, Clifford**
Opthamologist
Practice limited to eye
26 Boston St. . . . . . . . . . . . 389-7958

**Dorsey, Anne**
Ear, nose and throat
By appointment only
34 Congress St. . . . . . . . . . . 389-4612

**Drummond, Matt**
Practice limited to X-ray and
  radiology
36 Lynn St. . . . . . . . . . . . . . . 345-6867

**Eastern Allergy Associates**
Peter Davids
Joe Sands
Joseph DiCaro
Practice limited to allergy
Parkview Med. Bldg. . . . . . . 389-9005

**Faith, Paul**
Obstetrics and gynecology
By appointment only
24 Andover St. . . . . . . . . . . 345-1128

**Forrest, Nelson**
Urology and proctology
By appointment only
34 P.O. Square . . . . . . . . . 389-1564

**Gafferty, Edward**
Practice limited to internal medicine
  and cardiology
Office hours by appointment
92 Main St. . . . . . . . . . . . . . 389-0206

## List on the Board: Finding a New Doctor

*How do you find a doctor when you move to a new city or town? List on the board:*

# Going to a New Doctor

## With Your Partner:

*The first time you go to a new doctor, you fill out a health history form. Fill this one out. Then role-play visiting the doctor for a checkup. Ask the questions on this form.*

PATIENT INFORMATION

NAME _____ DATE OF BIRTH _____

ADDRESS _____ AGE _____

_____ PHONE ( ) _____

EMPLOYER'S NAME _____

EMPLOYER'S ADDRESS _____

BUSINESS PHONE ( ) _____ SOCIAL SECURITY NO. _____

NEAREST OF KIN _____ PHONE ( ) _____

ADDRESS _____

DRUG ALLERGIES ☐ YES ☐ NO IF YES, LIST _____

REFERRING PHYSICIAN _____

| INSURANCE COV. | IDENT. NO. | COV. CODE NO. | SUBSCRIBER'S NAME |
|---|---|---|---|
| BLUE SHIELD | | | |
| BLUE SHIELD | | | |
| MEDICARE | | | |

MEDICAID _____ PERSON NO. _____

AUTO ACCIDENT  DATE OF ACCIDENT _____ DATE OF DISABILITY _____

COMPENSATION  DATE OF ACCIDENT _____ DATE OF DISABILITY _____

OTHER _____

*Please read and sign below*

**INSURANCE AND PAYMENT RELEASE**
I hereby authorize the physician to release any information acquired in the course of medical examination or treatment for insurance claim filing and authorize that payment for services rendered to me by the doctor can be paid directly to him. Photostat of this authorization shall be considered as effective and valid as the original.

SIGNATURE _____

# Accidents and Emergencies

## Group Discussion

*With your group describe these accidents.*

| stairs |
| --- |
| roller skate |
| slip |
| fall |
| cast |
| broken ankle |

| barefoot |
| --- |
| nail |
| puncture |
| wash |
| tetanus shot |

| knife |
| --- |
| cut |
| bleed |
| wash |
| bandage |

iron
burn
cold water
burn ointment

bicycle
crash
tree
concussion
ambulance

## Questions for Conversation

1. Is there a hospital in your community? What is its name?

   _____

2. Does the hospital have an emergency room? What hours is it open?

   _____

3. Have you ever been there? Have you ever taken anyone here?

   _____

4. Does your insurance cover emergency care?

   _____

5. What would you do if you were the person injured in the pictures above?

   _____

6. What is the telephone number of the emergency room in your community? The ambulance? The police emergency?

   _____

# Hospital Signs

Have you ever seen these signs around the hospital? What does each one mean?

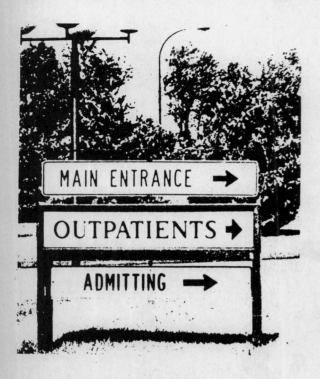

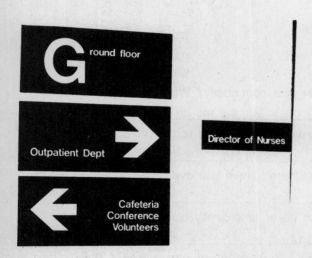

# Visiting the Dentist

*Write the correct sentence under each picture.*

| | |
|---|---|
| The patient is waiting to see the dentist. | The dentist has filled the patient's tooth. |
| The dentist is drilling the patient's tooth. | The dentist is giving the patient Novocain. |

## With Your Partner

*Ask your partner the questions.*

1. Do you go to the dentist?
2. What is your dentist's name? Where is your dentist's office?
3. Do you like your dentist?
4. Does your dentist give you Novocain? Gas? Sodium pentothal?
5. In your native country (or city) do people go to the dentist? What kind of fillings does the dentist use?

# 9

# Leisure

# Watching Television

## Picture for Discussion

What is happening in this picture? Do you ever watch T.V. and do something else at the same time? What?

## Find Someone Who

*Read this exercise with your teacher. Then find someone in your class who:*

1. watches the **news** on T.V. _____

2. watches **sports** on T.V. _____

3. watches **movies** on T.V. _____

4. likes **situation comedies** _____

5. likes **soap operas** _____

6. likes **game shows** _____

7. doesn't like to watch T.V. _____

8. watches **weather reports** on T.V. _____

9. doesn't like any **T.V. commercials** _____

10. watches T.V. late at night _____

## Class Discussion: T.V. Around the World

Tell the class about television in your native country. Do many people watch T.V.? Are T.V. sets expensive? How many hours a day are T.V. shows broadcast? What kinds of programs are there? Are there any commercials?

## Conversation Matrix: Favorites

*Write your name and the names of two classmates. Fill in the columns with your favorites.*

| | _____ | _____ | _____ |
|---|---|---|---|
| Favorite T.V. show | | | |
| Favorite comedian or comedienne | | | |
| Favorite actor or actress | | | |

## Class Activity

Use a T.V. guide or newspaper listing of programs. Find some favorite shows. What times are they on? What channels? What would be a good children's show? What would be a good show to learn English? Are there any shows in foreign languages?

# Movies

## Take a Poll

*Make a list on the board of the students' favorite movies. Ask how many students like each movie on the list. Which one is the class favorite?*

## Questions for Conversation

*Practice asking and answering these questions with your teacher. Then ask your partner the questions.*

1. Where is the closest movie theater?

   _____

2. What was the last movie you saw? What movie do you want to see?

   _____

3. How much does an admission ticket cost? Is it cheaper during the day?

   _____

4. Have you ever gone to a drive-in? Who did you go with?

   _____

5. Do you like to go to drive-ins? Why?

   _____

6. What kind of movies do you like? What is your favorite movie? Have you ever seen the same movie more than once?

   _____

7. Who is your favorite actor? Your favorite actress?

   _____

## Community Activity

1. Select a movie from the movie page. What time is it playing? Where is it playing?
2. Discuss the ratings of movies: What to do G, PG, PG-13, R, and X mean?

# Sports

## Find Someone Who

*First write the name of each sport. Then find someone in the class who likes the sport. Finally, choose one sport to tell the class about. Use the vocabulary lists next to the illustrations. Add other words to the lists.*

| | | |
|---|---|---|
| football | hockey | gymnastics |
| soccer | boxing | tennis |
| baseball | skiing | jogging |
| basketball | bowling | canoeing |

teams
bat
batter
diamond
stands
innings
home plate
base
_____
_____
_____

baseball

_____
*student's name*

court
basket
basketball
hoop
net
periods
_____
_____
_____

_____

_____

**136**

helmet
field
shoulder pads
cleats
football
half

_____

_____

_____

skis
ski poles
bindings
slope
trail
ski lift

_____

_____

_____

ring
gloves
round
referee

_____

_____

_____

puck
hockey stick
ice rink
skates
goal
periods

_____

_____

_____

canoe
paddle
river
current

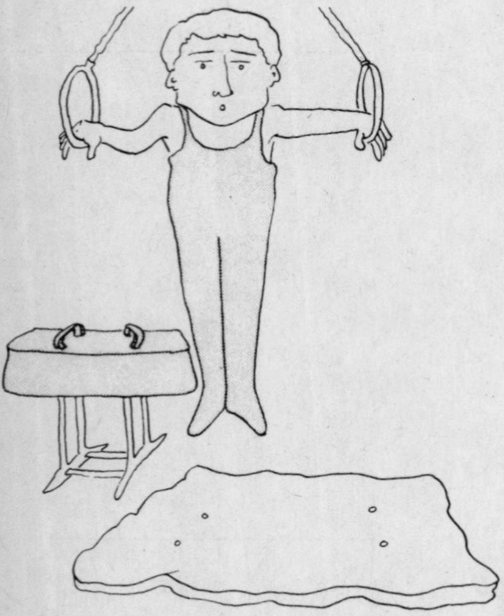

_____

_____

_____

rings
gymnast
pad
horse

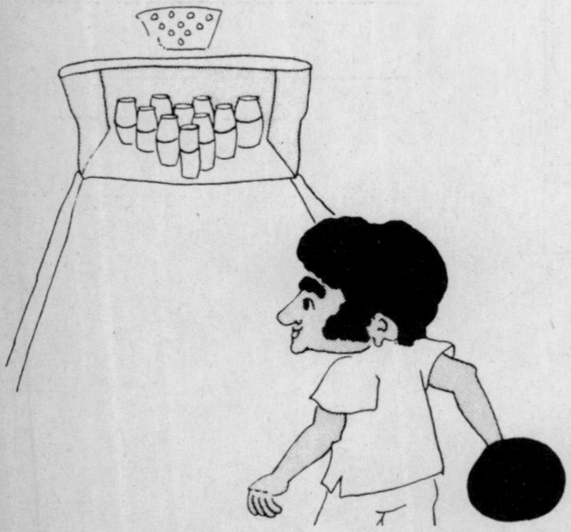

_____

_____

_____

alley
pins
gutter
spare
roll
string

_____

_____

_____

racquet
tennis ball
net
strings
serve

_____

_____

_____

sweat suit
running shoes
track
race
marathon

_____

_____

_____

soccer ball
goal
net
periods

_____

_____

_____

**139**

# Wild Animals

When you go camping, you may meet some of these wild animals:

1. Do any animals live near you? Which ones?

   _____

2. What animals live in your native country or city?

   _____

3. Have you ever seen any of *these* animals? Where have you seen them?

   _____

   _____

What should you do if you meet one of these animals?

# Camping

## With Your Class: Strip Story

*With your class, tell the story of this camping trip. Use the vocabulary list. Add vocabulary to the list.*

| | | |
|---|---|---|
| pack the car | campfire | hammock |
| hike | raccoon | _____ |
| tent | fishing | _____ |
| cookstove | lake | _____ |
| boots | mountain | _____ |
| lantern | mountain climbing | _____ |
| backpack | mountain goat | _____ |
| | set up camp | _____ |

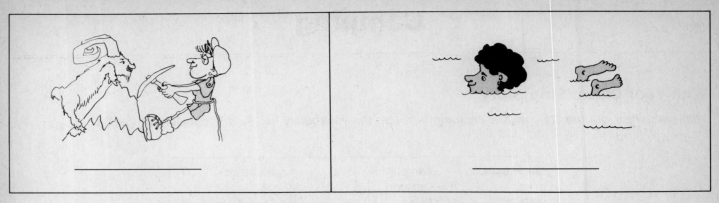

_____                    _____

_____

You tell the end

_____

Do people in your native country go camping? Where do they go? Is camping the same or different in the United States?

Send for camping information from your state or from a place you want to visit. Consult a camping atlas for sites near your destination. What facilities does the site have?

# Music

## Vocabulary

*Match these words with the correct instruments. Practice the vocabulary with your teacher. Does anyone in your class play any of these instruments?*

| | | | | |
|---|---|---|---|---|
| violin | trumpet | saxophone | accordion | trombone |
| piano | guitar | drums | flute | clarinet |

## Tell the Class: Instruments in Your Native Country

*Draw a picture on the board of an instrument in your native country. Tell the class about it.*

## With Your Partner

*Practice asking and answering these questions with your teacher. Then ask your partner the questions. Finally, report your interview to the class.*

1. Do you play a musical instrument? What instrument? What kind of music do you play? What is your favorite piece?
2. Do you like to sing? What type of songs? What is your favorite song?
3. What kinds of music do you like to listen to? Is there any kind of music you don't like to listen to?
4. What do you listen to music on? The radio? Tape cassettes? Records?
5. Who is your favorite singer?

## Class Activities

If you have a musical instrument, bring it in. Can you play something for the class?
Bring in a record or tape of songs in your native language or from a different region in your country.
Teach your favorite song to the class.

# Dance

## Questions for Conversation

1. Who likes to dance in your class? What kind of dances are popular?
2. Where do you go to dance? What kind of music do you like to dance to?
3. Do people in your native country dance a lot? What dances do they do? Are there any special dances for men? For women?
4. Do you like to watch other people dance? What kinds of dancing?

## Take a Poll: Favorite Dances

With your group, make a chart of the group's favorite dances. Report your results to the class. Make a master chart on the board of the class favorite dances.

| Name | Dance |
|------|-------|
|      |       |
|      |       |
|      |       |
|      |       |
|      |       |
|      |       |

## Picture for Conversation: Professional Dancing

What is happening in this picture? Do you like to watch ballet? What kinds of professional dancing are there in your native country?

## Class Activity:

Do you know a special dance? Teach it to the class. Bring music for the class to dance to.

# Going to School

## Questions for Conversation

1. What other courses can you take where you study English?
2. Have you ever taken another course? What was it? Tell the class about it.
3. Would you like to take another course? What kinds of courses are available? How much do they cost? What is the schedule?
4. Do many adults go to school in your native country (or city)? What kinds of courses do they take?

## Picture for Conversation: Success and Failure

What kind of class is this? What are the students doing? What happened? How do you think the people in this picture feel?

## Class Activity

Get a catalogue from an adult school. Pick out courses the students would like to take. Find the dates, times, and fees. How much English is required? Sign up and enjoy!

# Evaluation

## Writing Activity: Course Evaluation

At the end of many courses for adults in the United States, the teacher asks the students to evaluate the course and make suggestions for the future.

*Answer these questions for your teacher. Try to answer honestly. Your answers will help your teacher to plan for the next term.*

1. What was the best thing about this course?
2. What do you think your teacher should do the same way next term?
3. What do you think your teacher should change next term?
4. Do you think there should be more homework? Less homework? The same homework?
5. Do you think there should be more tests? Fewer tests? The same number of tests?

## With Your Group: Self-Evaluation

*In some courses, teachers ask students to evaluate their own learning. Answer these questions for yourself. Share your answers with your group and your teacher.*

1. What did you learn in this course?
2. Do you feel good about your effort in this course? If you could take the course again, would you study more? Less? The same amount? The same way?
3. How do you feel about your English now? What do you need to work on?

# Appendix

# Printing Upper-Case Letters
## (Capital Letters)

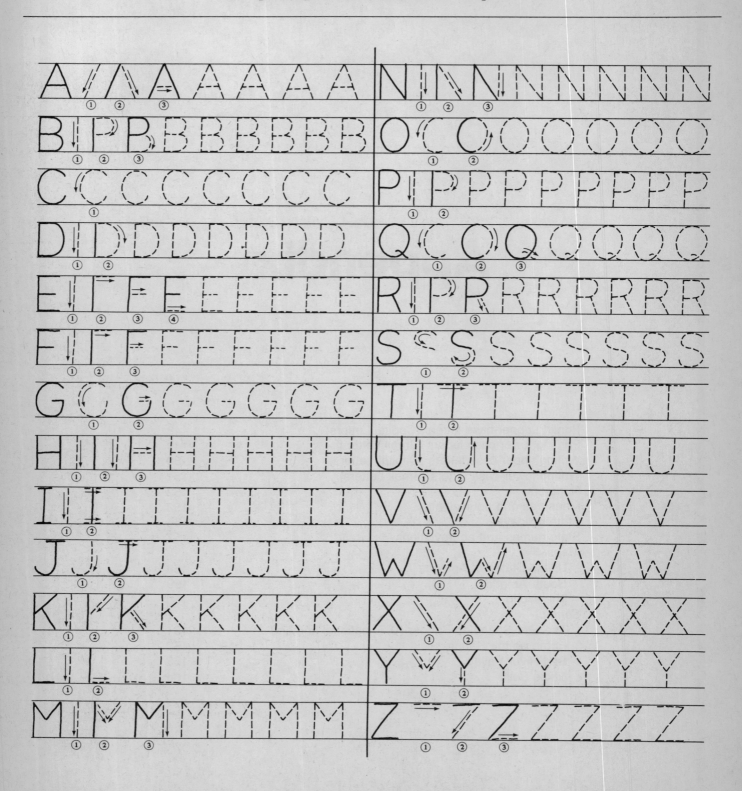

148

# Printing Lower-Case Letters
## (Small Letters)

a c o a a a a a a a    n n n n n n n n n n n

b b b b b b b b b b b    o c o o o o o o o o o o

c c c c c c c c c c c    p p p p p p p p p p p p

d o d d d d d d d d d    q o q q q q q q q q q

e e e e e e e e e e e    r r r r r r r r r r r r

f f f f f f f f f f f f    s s s s s s s s s s s s

g c o g g g g g g g g    t t t t t t t t t t t t t

h h h h h h h h h h h    u u u u u u u u u u u u

i i i i i i i i i i i i i i    v v v v v v v v v v v v

j j j j j j j j j j    w w w w w w w w w

k k k k k k k k k k    x x x x x x x x x x x x

l l l l l l l l l l l l l    y y y y y y y y y y y y

m m m m m m m m m m    z z z z z z z z z z z z

# Writing Upper-Case Letters
## (Capital Letters)

# Writing Lower-Case Letters
## (Small Letters)

a ... n
b ... o
c ... p
d ... q
e ... r
f ... s
g ... t
h ... u
i ... v
j ... w
k ... x
l ... y
m ... z

*A Writing Book: English in Everyday Life*, Tina Kasloff Carver, Sandra Douglas Fotinos, and Christie Kay Olson. Copyright © 1982. Reprinted by permission of Prentice-Hall, Inc.

# Numbers

## Cardinal Numbers

| | | | |
|---|---|---|---|
| 1 one | 26 twenty-six | | |
| 2 two | 27 twenty-seven | | |
| 3 three | 28 twenty-eight | | |
| 4 four | 29 twenty-nine | | |
| 5 five | 30 thirty | | |
| 6 six | 40 forty | | |
| 7 seven | 50 fifty | | |
| 8 eight | 60 sixty | | |
| 9 nine | 70 seventy | | |
| 10 ten | 80 eighty | | |
| 11 eleven | 90 ninety | | |
| 12 twelve | 100 one hundred | | |
| 13 thirteen | 200 two hundred | | |
| 14 fourteen | 300 three hundred | | |
| 15 fifteen | 400 four hundred | | |
| 16 sixteen | 500 five hundred | | |
| 17 seventeen | 600 six hundred | | |
| 18 eighteen | 700 seven hundred | | |
| 19 nineteen | 800 eight hundred | | |
| 20 twenty | 900 nine hundred | | |
| 21 twenty-one | 1,000 one thousand | | |
| 22 twenty-two | 10,000 ten thousand | | |
| 23 twenty-three | 100,000 one hundred thousand | | |
| 24 twenty-four | 1,000,000 one million | | |
| 25 twenty-five | | | |

## Ordinal Numbers

| | |
|---|---|
| first (1st) | twenty-sixth (26th) |
| second (2nd) | twenty-seventh (27th) |
| third (3rd) | twenty-eighth (28th) |
| fourth (4th) | twenty-ninth (29th) |
| fifth (5th) | thirtieth (30) |
| sixth (6th) | fortieth |
| seventh (7th) | fiftieth |
| eighth (8th) | sixtieth |
| ninth (9th) | seventieth |
| tenth (10th) | eightieth |
| eleventh (11th) | nintieth |
| twelfth (12th) | one hundredth |
| thirteenth (13th) | one thousandth |
| fourteenth (14th) | one millionth |
| fifteenth (15th) | |
| sixteenth (16th) | |
| seventeenth (17th) | |
| eighteenth (18th) | |
| nineteenth (19th) | |
| twentieth (20th) | |
| twenty-first (21st) | |
| twenty-second (22nd) | |
| twenth-third (23rd) | |
| twenty-fourth (24th) | |
| twenty-fifth (25th) | |

# Measures and Equivalents

## Conversions to Change

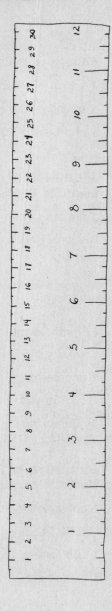

1. meters to yards, multiply the number of meters by 1.09.

2. yards to meters, multiply the number of yards by .91.

3. meters to inches, multiply the number of meters by 39.37

4. inches to meters, multiply the number of inches by .0254

5. millimeters to inches, multiply the number of millimeters by .04.

6. inches to millimeters, multiply the number of inches by 25.4.

7. kilometers to miles, multiply the number of kilometers by .62.

8. miles to kilometers, multiply the number of miles by 1.61.

9. liters to liquid quarts, multiply the number of liters by 1.06.

10. liquid quarts to liters, multiply the number of liquid quarts by 95.

11. liters to dry quarts, multiply the number of liters by .91.

12. dry quarts to liters, multiply the number of dry quarts by 1.1

13. kilograms to pounds, multiply the number of kilograms by 2.2.

14. pounds to kilograms, multiply the number of pounds by .45.

15. centimeters to inches, multiply the number of centimeters by .4.

16. inches to centimeters, multiply the number of inches by 2.54.

## Measure of Length

**Metric to English units:**

1 meter = 39.37 inches

= 3.28 feet

= 1.09 yards

1 centimeter = .4 inch

1 millimeter = .04 inch

1 kilometer = .62 mile

**English to metric units:**

1 inch = 25.4 millimeters

= 2.54 centimeters

= 0.254 meter

1 foot = .3 meter

1 yard = .91 meter

1 mile = 1.61 kilometers

## Measure of Capacity—liquid measure
**Metric to English units:**

1 liter = 1.06 liquid quarts

**English to metric units:**

1 liquid quart = .95 liter

## Measure of Capacity—dry measure
**Metric to English units:**

1 liter = .91 dry quart

**English to metric units:**

1 dry quart = 1.1 liters

## Measure of Weight

**Metric to English units:**

1 gram = .04 ounce

1 kilogram = 2.2 pounds

1 metric ton = 2204.62 pounds

**English to metric units:**

1 ounce = 28.35 grams

1 pound = .45 kilogram

1 short ton = .91 metric ton

## Measure of Area
**Metric to English units:**

1 square centimeter = .16 square inches

1 square meter = 10.76 square feet

= 1.2 square yards

1 square kilometer = .39 square miles

**English to metric units:**

1 square inch = 6.45 square centimeters

1 square foot = .09 square meter

1 square yard = .84 square meter

1 square mile = 2.59 square kilometers

## Measure of Volume
**Metric to English units:**

1 cubic centimeter = .06 cubic inch

1 cubic meter = 35.31 cubic feet

1 cubic meter = 1.31 cubic yards

1 liter = .04 cubic foot

## English to metric units:

1 cubic inch = 16.39 cubic centimeters

1 cubic foot = .03 cubic meter

1 cubic yard = .76 cubic meter

1 cubic foot = 28.32 liters

## English Measures

### weight

ounce (oz.)

   16 oz. = 1 lb.

pound (lb.)

### length

inch (in. or ")

   12" = 1'

foot (ft. or ')

   3' = 1 yd.

yard (yd.)

   1760 yds = 1 mi.

mile (mi.)

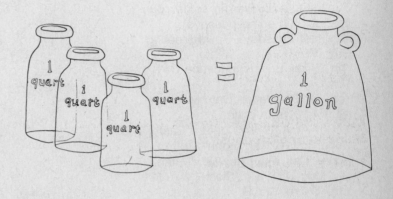

### liquid

pint (pt.)

   2 pts. = 1 qt.

quart (qt.)

   4 qts. = 1 gal.

gallon (gal.)

$\frac{1}{4}$ full    $\frac{1}{2}$ full    $\frac{3}{4}$ full    full

# State Holidays

January 6, Three Kings' Day: P.R.

January 8, Battle of New Orleans Day: La.

January 11, De Hostos' Birthday: P.R.

January 19, Robert E. Lee's Birthday: Ark., Fla., Ga., Ky., La., N.C., S.C., Tex.

January (third Monday), Robert E. Lee's Birthday: Ala., Miss. Lee-Jackson Day in Va.

January 30, F. D. Roosevelt's Birthday: Ky.

February or March (1 day before Ash Wednesday), Mardi Gras (Shrove Tuesday): Ala., Fla. (in some counties), La. (in some parishes).

March (first Tuesday), Town Meeting Day: Vt.

March 2, Texas Independence Day: Tex.

March 17, Evacuation Day: Mass. (Suffolk County only).

March or April (2 days before Easter), Good Friday: Cal. (noon–3 p.m.), Conn., Del., Fla., Hawaii, Ill., Ind., La., Md., N.D., Pa., Tenn. Wis. (11 a.m.–3 p.m.), P. R.

March or April (1 day after Easter), Easter Monday: N.C.

March 22, Abolition Day, P.R.

March 25, Maryland Day: Md.

March 26, Kuhio Day: Hawaii

March (last Monday), Seward's Day: Ark.

April 12, Halifax Resolutions Anniversary: N.C.

April 13, Thomas Jefferson's Birthday: Ala., Mo., Okla.

April 16, De Diego's Birthday: P.R.

April (third Monday), Patriot's Day: Me., Mass.

April 21, San Jacinto Day: Tex.

April 22, Arbor Day: Neb.

April 22, Oklahoma Day: Okla.

April (fourth Monday), Fast Day: N.H.

April (last Monday), Confederate Memorial Day: Ala., Miss.

April (last Friday), Arbor Day: Utah.

May (first Tuesday after first Monday), Primary Election Day: Iowa

May 4, Rhode Island Independence Day: R.I.

May 10, Confederate Memorial Day: N.C., S. C.

May 20, Mecklenburg Independence Day: N.C.

June (first Monday), Jefferson Davis' Birthday: Ala., Miss.

June 3, Jefferson Davis' Birthday: Ga., S.C., Tex., also called Confederate Memorial Day in Ky. and La.

June 9, Senior Citizens Day: Okla.

June 11, Kamehameha Day: Hawaii

June 14, Flag Day: Pa.

June 17, Bunker Hill Day: Mass. (Suffolk County)

June 20, West Virginia Day: W.V.

July 17, Muñoz Rivera's Birthday: P.R.

July 24, Pioneer Day: Utah

July 25, Constitution Day: P.R.

July 27, Barbosa's Birthday: P.R.

August (first Monday), Colorado Day: Colo.

August (second Monday), Victory Day: R. I.

August 16, Bennington Battle Day: Vt.

August (third Friday), Admission Day: Hawaii

August 30, Huey P. Long Day: La.

September 9, Admission Day: Cal.

September 12, Defender's Day: Md.

September 16, Cherokee Strip Day: Okla.

September (first Saturday after full moon), Indian Day: Okla.

October 10, Oklahoma Historical Day: Okla.

October (third Monday), Alaska Day: Alas.

October 31, Nevada Day: Nev

November 1, All Saints Day: La.

November 4, Will Rogers Day: Okla.

November 19, Discovery Day: P.R.

# State Names and Abbreviations

Alabama
(Ala. or AL)
Alaska (AK)
Arizona
(Ariz. or AZ)
Arkansas
(Ark. or AR)
California
(Calif. or CA)
Colorado
(Colo. or CO)
Connecticut
(Conn. or CT)
Delaware
(Del. or DE)
District of Columbia
(D.C. or DC)
Florida (Fla. or FL)
Georgia (Ga. or GA)
Hawaii (HI)
Idaho (ID)
Illinois (Ill. or IL)
Indiana (Ind. or IN)
Iowa (IA)
Kansas (Kans. or KS)
Kentucky (Ky. or KY)
Louisiana
(La. or LA)

Maine (Me. or ME)
Maryland (Md. or MD)
Massachusetts
(Mass. or MA)
Michigan
(Mich. or MI)
Minnesota
(Minn. or MN)
Mississippi
(Miss. or MS)
Missouri
(Mo. or MO)
Montana
(Mont. or MT)
Nebraska
(Nebr. or NB)
Nevada (Nev. or NV)
New Hampshire
(N.H. or NH)
New Jersey
(N.J. or NJ)
New Mexico
(N. Mex. or NM)
New York
(N.Y. or NY)
North Carolina
(N.C. or NC)
North Dakota
(N. Dak. or ND)

Ohio (OH)
Oklahoma
(Okla. or OK)
Oregon
(Oreg. or OR)
Pennsylvania
(Penna., Pa., or PA)
Rhode Island
(R.I. or RI)
South Carolina
(S.C. or SC)
South Dakota
(S. Dak. or SD)
Tennessee
(Tenn. or TN)
Texas (Tex. or TX)
Utah (UT)
Vermont (Vt. or VT)
Virginia (Va. or VA)
Washington
(Wash. or WA)
West Virginia
(W. Va. or WV)
Wisconsin
(Wis. or WI)
Wyoming
(Wyo. WY)

# United States of America

# South America

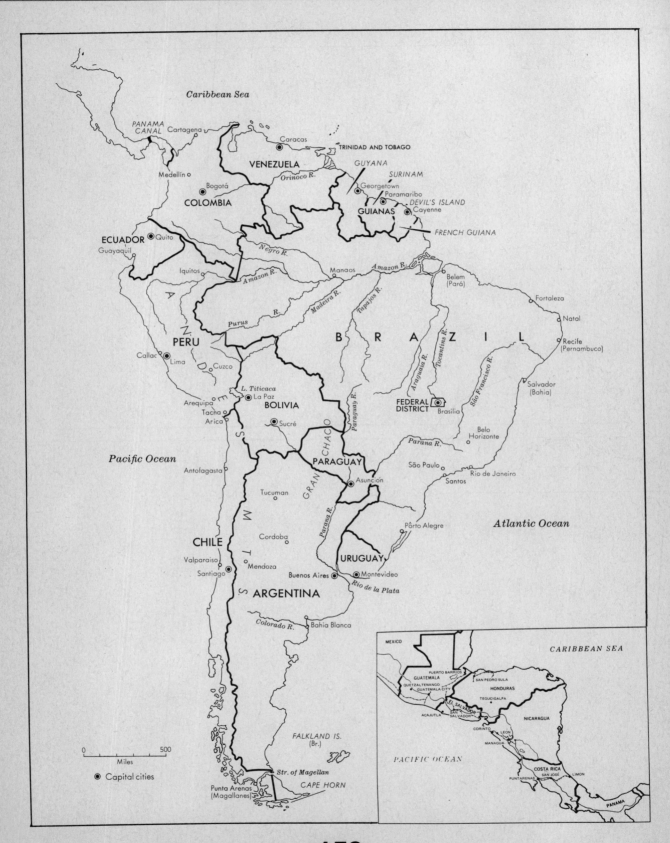

Caribbean Sea

PANAMA CANAL
Cartagena
Caracas
TRINIDAD AND TOBAGO
VENEZUELA
GUYANA
SURINAM
Medellín
Bogotá
Georgetown
Paramaribo
DEVIL'S ISLAND
COLOMBIA
Orinoco R.
GUIANAS
Cayenne
FRENCH GUIANA
ECUADOR
Quito
Guayaquil
Negro R.
Iquitos
Manaos
Amazon R.
Belem (Pará)
Amazon R.
Fortaleza
A
Purus
R.
Madeira R.
Tapajos R.
B  R  A  Z  I  L
Natal
PERU
Callao
Lima
Cuzco
Araguaia R.
Tocantins R.
São Francisco R.
Recife (Pernambuco)
L. Titicaca
Salvador (Bahia)
Arequipa
La Paz
BOLIVIA
FEDERAL DISTRICT
Brasilia
Tacna
Arica
Sucré
Paraguay R.
Belo Horizonte
Pacific Ocean
Parana R.
Antofagasta
GRAN CHACO
PARAGUAY
São Paulo
Rio de Janeiro
Tucuman
Asunción
Santos
Parana R.
Atlantic Ocean
Pôrto Alegre
CHILE
Cordoba
Valparaiso
Mendoza
URUGUAY
Santiago
Buenos Aires
Montevideo
ARGENTINA
Rio de la Plata
Colorado R.
Bahia Blanca

0      500
Miles

● Capital cities

FALKLAND IS. (Br.)

Str. of Magellan

CAPE HORN

Punta Arenas (Magallanes)

MEXICO
CARIBBEAN SEA
PUERTO BARRIOS
GUATEMALA
SAN PEDRO SULA
QUETZALTENANGO
HONDURAS
GUATEMALA CITY
TEGUCIGALPA
EL SALVADOR
ACAJUTLA
SAN SALVADOR
NICARAGUA
CORINTO
LEÓN
MANAGUA
PACIFIC OCEAN
COSTA RICA
PUNTARENAS
SAN JOSÉ
LIMON
PANAMA

**159**

# The World

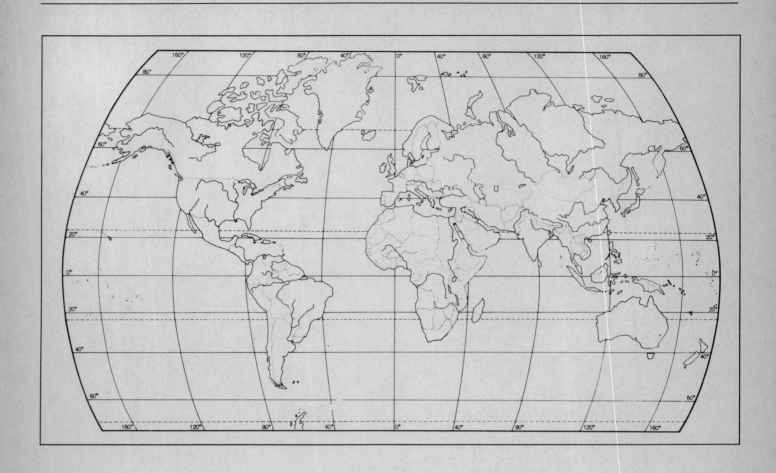

# The Star-Spangled Banner
# (U.S. National Anthem)

**Words by Francis Scott Key**

Oh, say can you see, by the dawn's early light,
What so proudly we hailed at the twilight's last gleaming?
Whose broad stripes and bright stars, thro' the perilous fight,
O'er the ramparts we watched were so gallantly streaming?
And the rocket's red glare, the bombs bursting in air,
Gave proof through the night that our flag was still there.

**Chorus:**

Oh say does that star-spangled banner yet wave
O'er the land of the free and the home of the brave?

On the shore dimly seen through the mist of the deep,
Where the foe's haughty host in dread silence reposes,
What is that which the breeze, o'er the towering steep,
As it fitfully blows, half conceals, half discloses?
Now it catches the gleam of the morning's first beam,
In full glory reflected, now shines on the stream;

**Chorus:**

'Tis the star-spangled banner! Oh long may it wave
O'er the land of the free and the home of the brave!

Oh, thus be it ever, when free-men shall stand
Between their loved homes and and the war's desolation,
Blessed with vict'ry and peace, may the heav'n rescued land
Praise the pow'r that hath made and preserved us a nation.
Then conquer we must, when our cause it is just,
And this be our motto, "In God is our trust!"

**Chorus:**

And the star-spangled banner in triumph shall wave
O'er the land of the free and the home of the brave!

# Home on the Range

Oh, give me a home, where the buffalo roam,
Where the deer and the antelope play;
Where seldom is heard a discouraging word,
And the skies are not cloudy all day.

**Chorus:**

Home, home on the range,
Where the deer and the antelope play;
Where seldom is heard a discouraging word,
And the skies are not cloudy all day.

How often at night when the heavens are bright
With the lights from the glittering stars;
Have I stood there amazed and I asked as I gazed
If their glory exceeds that or ours.

**Chorus:**

Home, home on the range,
Where the deer and the antelope play;
Where seldom is heard a discouraging word,
And the skies are not cloudy all day.

# Red River Valley

From this valley they say you are going,
We will miss your bright eyes and sweet smile,
For they say you are taking the sunshine,
That brightens our pathway awhile.

Come sit by my side if you love me,
Do not hasten to bid me adieu,
But remember the Red River Valley,
And the girl that has loved you so true.

# Jingle Bells

Dashing through the snow
In a one-horse open sleigh;
O'er the fields we go,
Laughing all the way.
Bells on bob-tail ring,
Making spirits bright,
What fun it is to ride and sing
A sleighing song tonight.

**Chorus:**

Jingle Bells! Jingle Bells!
Jingle all the way!
Oh, what fun it is to ride in a one-horse open sleigh!
Oh! Jingle Bells! Jingle Bells!
Jingle all the way!
Oh, what fun it is to ride in a one-horse open sleigh!

Day or two ago
I thought I'd take a ride,
Soon Miss Fanny Bright was seated by my side,
The horse was lean and lank,
Misfortune seemed his lot,
He got into a drifted bank,
And we, we got upsot!

**Chorus:**

Jingle Bells! Jingle Bells!
Jingle all the way!
Oh, what fun it is to ride in a one-horse open sleigh!
Oh! Jingle Bells! Jingle Bells!
Jingle all the way!
Oh, what fun it is to ride in a one-horse open sleigh!

Now the ground is white,
Go it while you're young!
Take the girls tonight, and sing this sleighing song.
Just get bobtailed bay,
Two forty for his speed,
Then hitch him to an open sleigh
And crack! You'll take the lead.

**Chorus:**

Jingle Bells! Jingle Bells!
Jingle all the way!
Oh, what fun it is to ride in a one-horse open sleigh.
Oh! Jingle Bells! Jingle Bells!
Jingle all the way!
Oh, what fun it is to ride in a one-horse open sleigh!